LADIES ON THE FIELD

TWO CIVIL WAR NURSES FROM MAINE
ON THE BATTLEFIELDS OF VIRGINIA

BY

LIBBY MACCASKILL AND DAVID NOVAK

Also "THE LADIES WHO WENT TO THE FIELD"
by Clara Barton (Signal Tree Edition)

Signal Tree Publications
Livermore. Maine

ISBN 0-9651858-1-8
PRINTED IN LEXINGTON, VIRGINIA, BY JIM DEDRICK

ACKNOWLEDGEMENTS

The authors thank Megan Fox, Librarian at the Graduate School of Management, Simmons College in Boston; the librarians at the Maine State Library and the Maine State Archives in Augusta; historians Mr. and Mrs. Brand Livingstone; the Special Collection Library at Duke University; the Maine Historical Society at Portland; the Bath Historical Society; the Southern Historical Collection, Wilson Library, the University of North Carolina, Chapel Hill; and the National Archives at Washington, D. C. These wonderful people and institutions made our work possible, even pleasurable.

LM
DN
1996

"The story of the war will never be fully or fairly written if the achievements of women in it are untold."

--Frank Moore, 1866

"The history of the nurses of the Civil War has been an almost unwritten one."

--Kate Scott, 1910

PREFACE

Some years after the Civil War, a visitor to the annual reunion of Union soldiers called the Encampment of the Grand Army of the Republic might have seen this sight: moving slowly among a group of old soldiers across a now peaceful and grassy battlefield, the figure of an old woman. Though clearly cherished by the veterans who hover around her as they walk, her demeanor is not that of wife or sister; it is that of comrade and veteran. She nods and points when the soldiers speak, and it is clear that, like them, she has seen this ground when it was the object of contest, torn by shot and shell, and soaked with blood.

Who is she? What is she doing in this place, among these men? If the visitor had turned to the old soldiers for an answer, they would have responded that in the wrinkled face of the old woman they still saw the strong and gentle person who had served beside them so long ago when they were all young. The woman they now walked with through memory had braved public opinion, government bureaucracy, disease, and cannon to be where the men lay sick and wounded. She was a Civil War nurse.

CIVIL WAR NURSE

". . . [S]he has discarded hoops. . . . [S]he has a stout servicable apron nearly covering her dress. . . ."

—FROM *Woman's Work in the Civil War*

* * * * *

". . . [A] steamer came alongside with 30 wounded men from a skirmish at the front the day before. I had just time to put on my working dress . . . when they were brought on board."

—HARRIET WHETTEN

CHAPTER I

INTRODUCTION

*"I am not accustomed to use the language of eulogy.
I have never studied the art of paying compliments to
women. But I must say that, if all that has been said
by orators and poets since the creation of the world
in praise of women was applied to the women of
America, it would not do them justice for their
conduct during this war. . . ."* --ABRAHAM LINCOLN

President Lincoln's wartime tribute to American women
was deserved. Women of all ages, North and South, made
countless difficult, even heroic, sacrifices during the years of the
American Civil War (1861-1865). They sent their sons,
husbands, brothers, friends and sweethearts to fight and suffer
and die on the battlefield, while they themselves remained at
home to endure deprivations and sorrows, sometimes extreme.

While the front was often in the very yards of women in
the South, for the most part the women of the North remained
far removed from the scenes of battle, on the Union homefront,
where they spent the worried and lonely war years struggling to
support and keep their families, their family businesses, and
farms. There were, however, hundreds of these Union women
who chose to go with the Army into the South, to serve in a way
not at all usual for the time--that is, as nurses.

It is hard for us to imagine now a time when, apart from
a few orders of Catholic nuns, there were no female nurses to
speak of, no well-trained military medics--male or female, no
Red Cross workers to take medical aid to soldiers on or near the

battlefield. But this was the case until a young woman named Florence Nightingale went to the Crimea in November of 1855 to do something about the horrors there, where the English army was in danger of collapsing because of the high rate of death from disease. She and the 37 Englishwomen who went with her to clean and nurse in the great English military hospital at Scutari drastically reduced the numbers of men dying from disease. But that great forward movement in military medical care had taken place only six years before the Civil War in America began--and within an army an ocean away--in a time when news and innovations did not travel fast.

Still, in the United States the medical establishment took note of Nightingale's precepts on sanitation and hygiene, and American women eagerly followed her advice on nursing as she set them down in her famous *Notes on Nursing*, in which Nightingale outlined her rules on sanitation in the sickroom. In this work she also asserted that "every woman is a nurse." But this was taken to apply only to the care of members of the household, in the home--at least it was if a woman wanted to be thought of as a decent and moral woman.

When the Civil War broke out, American women did not as a strict social rule nurse outside the home. After all, it had been only a few years since

> hospitals [had been] only places where one dumped the paupers who were ill, when, as Florence Nightingale said, she could find no nurses who were not drunkards, and few who did not carry on sexual intercourse in the wards with any male patient who wanted them. Those were the days when the nurses at Bellevue [H]ospital in New York City were described as "drunken prostitutes."

No, it was not acceptable for a woman to nurse professionally, and considered especially unacceptable would have been nursing in the (then) all-male military environment. Even the American doctor who had encouraged Nightingale in her nursing career, Dr. Samuel Gridley Howe, prevented his own wife, Julia Ward Howe, from entering the profession as a wartime volunteer. (Instead, she exhibited her patriotism in the lyrics of *The Battle Hymn of the Republic*.) Seeing to the most intimate details of caring for sick and wounded men who were not close family members was simply not done by any woman who wanted to be well regarded. The age was one of acute sensibilities--an age when a "lady" did not dare show her ankle, never mind letting the world know she had undressed men, bathed even the most private of wounds on their bodies, and seen to their most personal medical needs. In addition, it was sincerely believed that women were emotionally unsuitable for war work, that they would run at the sound of shooting, or faint at the sight of blood. As it turned out there was good cause to worry about the latter; the Civil War battlefield was a scene of enormous carnage. "I ride over the battlefield," one soldier wrote, ". . . National and Confederates, young, middle-aged, and old, are scattered over the woods and fields for miles . . . men with their legs shot off; one with brains scooped out with cannon ball; another with a half a face gone; another with entrails protruding. . . ."

In 1910 Kate M. Scott, National Secretary of the Civil War nurses association, remembered the age:

> It can scarcely be realized [now], when the Glorious Red Cross, with its perfect system of trained nurses, has made the vocation of a nurse an honorable one, when our Government is employing women as nurses, what nerve and patriotic devotion it took for the young woman

of the [eighteen-]sixties to brave public opinion
and enlist for the hospital and field service.

Today the names of but a very few of the women who,
in spite of all, did go to war are familiar to us: Louisa May
Alcott, Clara Barton, and Dorthea Dix come to mind. And yet
it is for her novels that we remember Louisa May Alcott--not for
her months as a nurse in a Union hospital in Washington. And
when we think of Clara Barton, we are more likely to think of
her role in the founding of the American Red Cross than we are
to think of her leading her precious wagons of supplies onto a
desperate field of war. Dorthea Dix was a stalwart reformer and
feminist who herself did not want to be remembered for her
work as Civil War nursing superintendent.

It is a sad and terrible oversight that more of the names
of the selfless, brave women who went to war to alleviate
suffering are not known. It is sometimes said that we are a
country in need of real heroes and heroines. But this is not true;
we have thousands. We only need to recognize them.

Two of these heroines were women from Maine:
Isabella Fogg and Sarah Sampson. These are women who
should be as well known to us today as, for example, Clara
Barton--indeed, as well known as many of the great Union
generals of the Civil War. For they were, like Barton, war
nurses, brave and dedicated people whose actions and even very
presence in the hospitals and on or near the battlefields were
crucially important to the well-being and probably the very
survival of the army. And yet today they remain relatively
unknown, even in their home state of Maine, overshadowed by
the commanders whose men they ministered to--overlooked not
necessarily because they were women; the famous Florence

Nightingale was a woman--but mostly because the great, convulsive struggle of their time was represented by the army and its commanders.

When the "rebellion" (as it came to be known in the North) first arose, the small Medical Department of the United States Army was not considered a priority. At the time it consisted of a mere 98 doctors (as opposed to 11,000 at the end of the war), and the largest army hospital contained 40 beds--and was located at Fort Leavenworth, Kansas, far from most of the fighting. Care of the sick and wounded had never been a primary or even what might be called a secondary concern of the army anyway, and since popular wisdom held that the rebellion would be easily suppressed--within a few weeks at most--the North was unwilling and unprepared to restructure its medical organization to meet needs it did not foresee. When in April of 1861 President Lincoln called for 75,000 troops to serve for three months, there were no provisions in place to remove any of these soldiers who might be sick or wounded from the field, or, once they had been somehow removed, to take care of them in any medically sound way. Little provision had been made for medicines, or bedding, or even replacement clothing. And there was certainly no provision made for nursing. Even before the first significant battle, that of First Bull Run (First Manassas), in July of 1861, mustered soldiers--crowded into dirty and disease-ridden army camps--suffered miserably from illness, with only convalescent soldiers as nurses to their fellow comrades. And for some time after First Bull Run conditions remained almost unbelievably terrible in the "regimental hospitals." One prominent female Civil War nurse, Mary Livermore (well known in her day) described these places as being "carriage houses" and "sheds"

> . . . [which] compressed within their narrow
> limits more filth and discomfort, neglect and

[5]

suffering, than would have sufficed to defile and demoralize ten times as much space. The fetid odor of typhoid fever, erysipelas, dysentery, measles, and healing wounds, was rendered more nauseating by unclean beds and unwashed bodies. . . .
The nurses were convalescent soldiers, wan, thin, weak, and requiring nursing themselves; and though they were kind to their comrades, they were wholly worthless as nurses.

The attitude of the US Army, of *any* Western army of the day, was that the wounded, like the dead, were just so many pieces of disabled, and thereby useless, military materiel. A young female nurse assigned in the first months of the war to a hospital boat bitterly noted that "the principle of active war is, and perhaps must be, every marching man is precious; when he drops, he's a dog." And another nurse commented after almost two years in the field--upon visiting one of those "miserable holes called hospitals"--that she had found ". . . nothing, nothing but indifference. When a man is sick, no longer effective as a soldier, what does [the] government care for him?"

As soon as Fort Sumter was fired upon on April 12, 1861, women throughout the North began to gather in one another's parlors and in community halls to do what they could for the Cause within the strictures of their environment: they scraped at old linen with sharp knives to raise lint for packing wounds; they cut out and sewed shirts by hand; they baked and canned and put in barrels and boxes whatever useful they could find and spare.

As their informal clubs and church committees grew and

expanded into larger organizations capable of collecting very large numbers of supplies, the women came to require a reliable method of getting these supplies to the front. With this aim in mind, local ladies' relief societies formed; in fact the first of these was organized by the women of Bridgeport, Connecticut, on April 15, the very day President Lincoln called for those first 75,000 troops. Ultimately the Christian Commission (an offshoot of the YMCA), the Western Sanitary Commission (for the army in the West), and the United States Sanitary Commission (forerunner of the Red Cross) formed to organize the various relief societies, all to assist the Medical Department of the Army. Communities wanted their soldiers cared for, and the states took a particular interest in the troops of their own regiments. In Maine, the Maine Camp Hospital Association was formed for the specific benefits of the soldier-sons of that state.

All over the Union, women responded to the needs of the soldiers. Of all the needs, the most compelling were often those of the sick and wounded, and when the urge to care for such men was strengthened by a sense of adventure, patriotism, and perhaps above all concern for a particular loved one, it was not easily denied. Isabella Fogg was a 37-year-old widow from Calais, Maine, when her 19-year-old son's enlistment prompted her own; Sarah Sampson, from Bath, was a young wife who went to care for the men in her husband's regiment. These were two women who, in spite of the social and physical risks, had been moved to action by the events of their age and their own particular connection to them. They went, as one of their contemporaries noted, "very *early* to the Front, *before* prejudice yielded to humanity and when there was much opposition to a *lady's* ministering upon the field. . . ."

So in spite of public and private restrictions, hundreds of women, North and South, volunteered as nurses during the Civil War. The United States Sanitary Commission and the Medical Department of the Army tried to formulate regulations to provide

[7]

for women who wanted to serve in this way. Dorthea Dix, well known before the war for her work for and with the insane, was put in charge of selecting the women who would be official army nurses. It is generally conceded that to some extent she made a muddle of it. Dix had strict rules about age and appearance. As one former nurse later explained: "The women must be over thirty years of age, plain almost to repulsion in dress, and devoid of personal attractions, if they hoped to receive the approval of Miss Dix." Dix also made it very clear that her nurses were to stay in the general hospitals based in the cities: they were not to go to the field. Though the nurses she chose were generally good, such qualifications, though eventually loosened, caused some to be turned away who might have been effective, while at the same time compelling her to select others who turned out to be not very competent.

Even so, Dix offered a sense of approval and thus some protection for women who, in the face of public disapproval, wanted to serve. "No Lady," Civil War nurse Katharine Wormeley wrote, "should attempt to come [to nurse] unless accepted or otherwise appointed by the Government or the Commission. Ardent women with a mission should not come in any other way *if they value their respectability*" [emphasis added]. But even the aegis of a relief agency or commission did not guarantee protection from criticism. ". . . I cannot give up this work while I can be of any use," one young nurse serving with the United States Sanitary Commission wrote home in May of 1862. "Your disapprobation has been a great trial to me."

After the war, Clara Barton confessed that she had "struggled long and hard with [her] sense of propriety." "Whispering in one ear," she said, "was the appalling fact that I was a woman . . . and groans of suffering men, dying like dogs, unfed and unsheltered . . . thundering in the other." (She was ashamed, she added, that she "ever thought of such a thing.") Another emotionally torn Civil War nurse summed up

[8]

the position she and others (such as Clara Barton) found themselves in when she wrote that she had to stand

> firm against the tide of popular opinion, hearing
> myself pronounced demented--bereft of usual
> common sense; doomed to the horrors of an
> untended death--suffering torture, hunger, and
> the untold miseries of a soldier' fate; above all
> the loud echoed cry, "It is no place for a woman.
> . . ."

But she along with other "ardent women with a mission" (and brave, hardy souls they must have been) took it upon themselves to go, sometimes without official connection, pass, or permission, to the field, determined to be where the wounded were and to take care of them there. In the end, not only Dix's "approved" women served, but also "[s]cores of young maidens and matrons who had seen their loved ones march to the front, offered their services independently and were enrolled by surgeons, generals, and colonels of regiments, serving without pay. . . ."

Who were they? What kind of women went to be nurses in the Civil War? For the most part they were women who had no cause to promote other than that of mother, wife, sister, friend, and patriot. It is truly unfortunate that few first-hand accounts of their experiences exist, so unusual and important they are. And, also unfortunate, when women did write about what they had done, those sensibilities of the Victorian Age already mentioned served to deny us many of the details of what nursing on or near a battlefield entailed. The most famous of nurses' records today is that of a male nurse,

Walt Whitman (who agreed with Dix that women, unless they were "the motherly" sort, did not belong on the wards). His *Specimen Days* is perhaps followed in fame by Louisa May Alcott's *Hospital Notes*. Several other women wrote their nursing memoirs, but few of these were ever widely in print. Overwhelmingly, these women were not interested in making names for themselves, but simply in alleviating suffering when and where they could.

We can, however, gain some important insights about Civil War nurses from official reports, daily journals and personal letters, though only a relative few of any of these exist. As Isabella Fogg herself explained, "I kept no daily journal. Several times my hasty *notes* . . . were all lost, and on many occasions when a journal would have been most deeply interesting, I had no time. . . ." Fortunately, Isabella sent official letters, some of which are available in archives, and Sarah Sampson provided a (severely) condensed account of her experiences for the 1864-1865 [Maine] *Adjutant General's Report*. It is also helpful that some important pieces of personal information have survived from other sources, such as informal testimonies from former patients. The following is from a letter written shortly after the war by one soldier; in this passage he writes about one of the several nurses known to the troops simply as "Mother":

> . . . [W]e was an awful dirty set . . . and she washed us and cut our hair and fixed our wounds as good as any Dr. Yes and I saw her clean the worms and blood and matter off a fellows stump of his leg when it smelt so bad we had to hold our noses. . . .
>
> . . . [A]t Gettysburg she got there just after the battle and she dressed wounds from morning to night. . . . [A]t Chancellorsville she

was dressing the wounds just like any Dr. while they were fighting. . . . I tell you the boys think a heap of a woman that will come and suffer all that to do them good. . . .

So even without complete records, we can draw some conclusions about these women who went to war, about who they were and why they went. They were perhaps more adventurous than most other women of their day, perhaps stronger in some ways (not necessarily physically; several died, and many others went home completely broken down), but at heart much like their at-home counterparts. In fact, we find in their personal journals and in the letters they wrote home reason to believe that very often the overriding reasons for their actions were simply those of the ordinary wife, friend, sister, or mother:

And so the women . . . came to tend the sick and wounded. Untrained, motivated by a variety of intentions, many brought to their activity the preconceptions that had been so much a part of their domestic lives. Imbued . . . with notions of woman's maternal calling, mission of homemaker, and responsibility as a bringer of refinement, tenderness, and gentility to a male-dominated society, they in many cases approached the military hospital as an extension of home and the patients as their "boys."

No wounded or ill man in need, no matter what division or regiment he served, was neglected where these women worked. In the end it did not even matter to these nurses what army a man might belong to. Their enemies were wounds and disease, lack of medicine and food, inadequate shelter and clothes for their patients. Wounded and sick Rebel soldiers, once they came under the care of the Northern nurses, became nothing more nor less than men who needed help. While carrying food to a wounded Confederate, one young nurse was stopped by a Union soldier who said, "He's a Rebel; give that to me." Her response, "But a wounded man is our brother," caused both men to touch their caps in salute.

As for what the men thought of the nurses, one former soldier-patient very probably spoke for the great majority of them when he wrote:

> We hardly knew whether they were young or old; whether they had black tresses, auburn ringlets, or chestnut-brown curls; whether their eyes were blue, black, or hazel. It was enough that they were women. Their presence was proof that women cared for us, and were willing to brave dangers, and even come within range of the fearful shells to minister to those from whose wounds the warm blood was still flowing. In their presence, men could suffer with more fortitude, and die with more resignation. If we could not look upon our own dear ones at home, we could look upon their representatives.

Isabella Fogg and Sarah Sampson are only two of the many, many women who felt somehow called to service in the name of home, community, and country. They were two women from Maine whose courage was surpassed only by their capacity to care.

CHAPTER II

A MAINE MOTHER AT WAR
The Civil War Story of
ISABELLA MORRISON FOGG

Whispered low the dying soldier, pressed her hand and
faintly smiled:
'Was that pitying face his mother's? Did she watch
beside her child?'
Every voiceless word with meaning her woman's heart
supplied,
With her kiss upon his forehead, 'Mother!' murmured
he and died.

--ANONYMOUS

She was a middle-aged widow, and he was her teenaged son. Had there been no Civil War in America, they would have very likely quietly lived out their natural lives in the seaport lumber town called Calais on the downeast coast of Maine.

But there was a Civil War, and it changed the course of their lives as fundamentally as it did the course of American history.

Her name was Isabella Morrison Fogg, and she was born in December of 1823 in Scotch Ridge, near St. Stephens, in New Brunswick, the daughter of immigrants from Scotland. We know little about her life before 1861, but the sparse records reveal what must have been a rather difficult existence, growing up as she did on a hardscrabble farm. She was apparently very bright, for in spite of what must have been severe limitations to her educational opportunities, her recorded thoughts are intelligent and articulate; at one point in her life she even composed poetry.

ISABELLA MORRISON FOGG
CIVIL WAR NURSE

In 1837, when she was almost 14, Isabella married William Fogg and sometime afterwards moved to Calais, across the border in Maine, where she worked as a tailoress in a rented shop in which was also employed a seamstress; it was, presumably, a fairly active business, which she devoted herself to probably after becoming widowed. When the Civil War began, Isabella was 37 years old, and the one child of her three about whom we have any information (it is assumed the others did not survive childhood), a son named Hugh, was 19. From a wartime photograph portrait made of her in Washington, D.C., we know that Isabella was an attractive woman, with dark hair, kind, intelligent eyes, and a determined mouth.

Frank Moore, her earliest biographer, provides the following introduction to his version of her story:

> When the boom of the great guns in Charleston harbor, in the spring of 1861, went rolling across the continent, their echo penetrated to the border town of Calais, in Maine, on the extreme eastern verge of the Union, and there summoned men from their ships, and lumber mills, and farms, to the heroic duty of sustaining the government, threatened by a half continent in arms against it. . . . Nor did that summons reach the ears of men only. [Isabella Fogg] . . . felt that she also was called [by] a mingled cry of agony and of shame over the land. . . .

There is no doubt that Isabella Fogg was a patriot in the best nineteenth-century sense of the word, a woman whose heart belonged firmly to the Union, so there is probably more than a small element of truth in Moore's dramatic account. But it is more likely that Isabella's primary reason for leaving her home in Calais for the hospitals of the front was her son Hugh's

FORT SUMTER

enlistment. Understandably, worry over her soldier-son was probably as much a factor, if not more, than "a mingled cry of agony and shame over the land" in Isabella's decision to go to the war. In April of 1861, the month and year that her young, dark-haired, gray-eyed son Hugh joined the local militia, Isabella Fogg offered her services, without compensation, to the governor and the surgeon general of Maine.

We can only imagine what went through Isabella's mind when 60 of the young men of Calais began mustering under the persuasive leadership of local lumber surveyor Captain Joel Haycock, and she realized that Hugh, all seemingly left to her in the world, would be joining them. Did she protest? We cannot know. Isabella Fogg was not a woman afraid to speak her mind, but enlisting was widely considered the patriotic, right thing to do, and difficult to object to. It is, however, safe to assume that she was alarmed and worried. Hugh was, at 19, more than six years younger than the average age (25-26 years) of these Calais soldiers-to-be. The "boys" who went to war from Calais in Haycock's Company D were, in fact, men. In addition to their maturity they had on average the build of the woodsmen many of them were. The *Portland Advertiser* called them "a splendid set of men--of more than average stature, selected mostly from the hardy lumbermen and outdoor businessmen of that section." And one of the community leaders from Calais responsible for raising the regiment to which these men would eventually belong wrote of them: "They are large men in this battalion and remarkably well behaved." At five feet, four-and-a-half inches, Hugh Fogg was considerably smaller than the lumberjacks and mill hands who made up the largest part of the company, and his prewar job, that of a house servant, had not prepared him for the rough life of the army.

While we cannot know exactly what was in her heart, Isabella must have felt, in the end, that uncomfortable sweet anguish so often present in the homes of soldiers: that curious blend of pride, sorrow, and fear.

No doubt she was at the dock when on the rainy morning of May 21, 1861, Company D sailed away from Calais, the men dressed in shirts and trousers provided by the town, perhaps some even sewn by Isabella. And doubtless she saw the flags flap in the rain-driven breeze and the churning of the gray-green water of the inlet; and she would have heard the patriotic music of the Calais Brass Band as the men, Hugh among them, marched onto the gangplank of the steamer *Queen*.

When Company D, as part of the Sixth Maine (organized on July 15, 1861, to serve three years) finally left Portland, Maine, for the front on July 18, 1861--only three days before the Battle of First Bull Run (First Manassas)--Isabella was undoubtedly there, too, among the crowds of people, many from Calais, to say her goodbyes to Hugh; she had been in Portland for weeks collecting supplies and making other preparations for her own service.

In the fall of 1861 Isabella attached herself to one of the Maine regiments leaving for Annapolis. That fall and winter saw many of the Union soldiers in the area of Washington, D.C., and Annapolis ill with diseases common to crowded and unsanitary conditions such as those found in the army camps at that time. Typhoid hit them especially hard. Many from the Maine regiments fell ill with this, and Isabella stayed several months at Annapolis taking care of those men too sick to return to camp. She spent long days and nights, often with little relief, in the fever wards; it was an opportunity to look after other mothers' sons, and also a practical introduction to what lay ahead for her.

When the Union losses of the spring of the following year (1862) produced terrible numbers of wounded, and the rains and poor food resulted in great numbers of sick, Isabella went to the offices of the Sanitary Commission in Washington to offer her services. The Sanitary Commission was the chief agency in charge of supplying nurses to the hospital transports, and Isabella was assigned to spend the month of May on the hospital transport *Elm City* on the York and James Rivers, tending the sick and wounded on board. Hugh had been in the field since January of 1862, and during this time the Sixth Maine--by then known for good reason as the "Fighting Sixth"--had seen action at Yorktown, Lee's Mills, and Williamsburg. The numbers of wounded were overwhelming. As Moore tells it, "The mutilated heroes of Williamsburg were brought in one great, bloody cargo of suffering humanity--to the northern hospitals, on the *Elm City*. . . ."

Toward the end of May, the Sixth had reached the Chickahominy near Richmond:

> On the last day of May came the bloody field of Fair Oaks, after which there was a broad and unbroken stream of the wounded and sick pouring steadily to the rear from the active and warlike front, along the Chickahominy and around Richmond. The charge of these removals was in the hands of Dr. Swinburne, who observing the skill and activity of Mrs. Fogg in attending those who were brought on the cars to the White House, asked her if she would be willing to go up to the front and labor [with the Sanitary Commission] . . . Her prompt reply was, "That is just where I would like to go."

Throughout the month of June, 1862, while the Sixth Maine saw marching and fighting Isabella worked at a place called Savage Station, which was just two miles from the front at Fair Oaks. It was a very hot June, and Isabella, like many of the men from Maine, was not used to the unrelenting sun of the

HOSPITAL TREE AT FAIR OAKS

This idealized depiction of wounded was for the homefront.

THE REALITY OF THE WOUNDED

South; as she worked without rest she wore a wet towel tucked into her hat to protect herself from sunstroke. Toward the end of the fighting at Fair Oaks, just before the Seven Days' Battle, Hugh arrived from the extreme front to see his mother and to tell her about the horrible suffering of the men of the Sixth Maine. The next morning Isabella was on her way to them through the "Chickahominy Swamp" (White Oak Swamp) in a wagon loaded with supplies.

At their camp, she found troops by the score suffering from typhoid fever, and no shelter or medicine to speak of. She returned to Savage Station that evening and made plans to do more for these men: meanwhile, however, the Confederates had won the battle at Gaines' Mill (Cold Harbor), and Savage Station with its thousands of sick and wounded was ordered abandoned. Risking capture, Isabella could not bring herself to leave until the very last moment before the retreat to Harrison's Landing (at Berkeley Plantation on the James River). From her ambulance, she did what she could for the men on the way during that terrible, stormy night in early July of 1862. And she continued to nurse at the landing, leaving only occasionally to go into the field to tend to soldiers remaining there.

Besides typhoid fever, malaria ("Chickahominy Fever") struck the Sixth Maine badly in the summer of 1862, and evidently Hugh was one of its victims. He and many others were to spend long months away from their regiment, recovering in the general hospitals in and around Washington. According to one member of the Sixth, the men who fell ill were not shirkers but "some of the very best men. . . ."

When the Union army began its retreat from Harrison's Landing to the Potomac in August, Isabella Fogg travelled with the steamer *Spaulding*, full of sick and wounded, to the army hospital in Philadelphia. Then she returned to Maine for some much needed rest. She had been gone a year from her home state.

While in Portland, Isabella wrote letters to the governor and spoke to the mayor of the city about the situation at the front and the need to do something about it. In September she met with members of a "ladies' committee" of the Free Street Baptist Church of Portland, a group which had been sending supplies to the soldiers with somewhat limited success: bureaucratic red tape had kept most of what had been collected locked up in Portland's Custom House, and of the material they had managed to send south, boxes had been broken into, and clothing and food stolen. Fogg and another volunteer nurse named Harriet Eaton offered to take the contributions to the front themselves, to make certain that they arrived safely into the hands of those they were meant for--that is, the men of the Maine regiments. The Ladies' Committee along with some influential men of the community accepted the nurses' offer, and the resulting agreement between Fogg and Eaton, the Ladies' Committee, and the community leaders was to be called the Maine Camp Hospital Association. It was to prove to be one of the most effective organizations of its kind in the Civil War. In its own words, its stated origin and purpose were that

> [i]t having been represented during the latter part of 1862, that there was much suffering among the soldiers of the Potomac army, not reached by any other organization then at work, and as there were at that time ten Maine Regiments in that Department, it was resolved by a few gentlemen and ladies at the residence of the late Hon. Jedediah Jewett [*a former mayor of Portland*], on the evening of Nov. 17, to form a Society to labor more particularly among the Maine Regiments, and to be called the Maine

THE LADIES WITH THEIR PRECIOUS SUPPLIES FROM THE PEOPLE AT HOME

"The ties of neighborhood, kindred, and human nature unite to bind upon us the high obligation to care for and cherish the devoted men who 'do and dare' for the country . . . who have gone *forth for us* to battle with the rebellion. Be it our part to sustain their hands while they strive with the enemy. . . ."

—FROM "To the People of Maine"

Camp Hospital Association.

Two ladies then on the field were asked to distribute such stores as we might be able to forward to them, which they kindly consented to do. . . .

Isabella M. Fogg was one of the "two ladies then on the field." Though these women were instructed to "particularly" help soldiers from Maine, they were also "instructed to administer to all whom they can give relief, of whatever nationalities, States, grades or colors; whenever a soldier is found sick or wounded to give him help."

In October of 1862, to the strains of soldiers "singing 'Glory Halleluyah,'" Isabella Fogg set out once again for the South, "following the flag" into Virginia in company of the advancing army; her duty now was to see to the needs of Maine soldiers at Harper's Ferry and other places near the front. With her was Harriet Eaton, whose mind, like Isabella's, was very "much on [her] dear soldier boy," her son Frank, who--like Hugh--was in the army. And accompanying them both was Colonel Hathaway, the State Agent of the Maine Camp Hospital Association, whose job it was to see that the supplies sent by the relief agency reached their destination. The men at Harper's Ferry were the wounded from "bloody" Antietam (Sharpsburg), a battle which had taken place in mid-September of 1862 and in which Hugh's unit had participated, though Hugh himself was at the time hospitalized in Washington, and (undoubtedly to Isabella's great relief) away from the fighting. Hugh would remain hospitalized for months.

In a letter to Colonel Hathaway, Isabella wrote the following account of her visit to the field:

. . . Here the sick are in a fearful condition, in every old house and church and hundreds on the

[25]

WASHINGTON AND VICINITY

ground. . . . We visited the sick of the 19th in care of Dr. Hawes, asst. surgeon, he has upwards of 50, does all in his power for their comfort. . . . [W]e went over to Loudon Valley to learn the condition of several hundreds who had been sent the day previous without any preparation. We found them lying about on the ground, in all directions, many convalescent, but a great many *very low.* At this time no surgeons, nurses or cooks were on the ground. . . . After[wards] . . . we left for Berlin, and here the misery and suffering beggars all description, the heart sickens at the sight. . . . Taking a stroll through the town, we searched every old school house, log cabin &c. for the poor men who had been left behind, as our army moved on.

On the same day that Isabella was writing to Hathaway about her experiences ministering to the Maine men after Antietam, Chaplain George Knox, then of the 10th Maine, was writing to the Maine Camp Hospital Association in Portland:

Seeing [Mrs. Fogg and Mrs. Eaton] so successful, I desire to inform you that the doubts which I expressed . . . are entirely dispelled; and I would earnestly encourage those now engaged in this labor of love and patriotism to a patient continuance in well doing. I have not time to give you even a few from the multitude of facts bearing on this subject. Could you have been here during the last two or three weeks, you would have had most ample proof of the need of just such persons as you have sent, and just such labor as they are performing.

[27]

Although Isabella Fogg had set out in the company of Harriet Eaton and was to work with her on behalf of the Maine Camp Hospital Association, there was apparently some difficulty with this arrangement. In his own letter to Colonel Hathaway, Mr. C. C. Hayes, the Assistant State Agent traveling with Eaton and Fogg, alluded to the problem: "I find," he wrote, "that Mrs. Fogg works away from Mrs. Eaton much better than with her and for the future I shall endeavor to have their labors so divided that they can work in two different regiments. . . . Mrs. Eaton has gone to the 2nd [Maine], Mrs. Fogg to the 20th [Maine]."

There are some who believe that a rift occurred because Isabella was sensitive to the fact that her Calais roots were looked down upon by ladies of Portland such as Eaton; others believe the trouble was caused by interfering third parties. There is also evidence that Fogg's strong opinions and willful personality might have been responsible. There is no doubt that the two women approached their war work very differently and did not appreciate one another's perspective. But whatever the problem was and whoever caused it, it is revealing that Hayes put his own health in Isabella's hands. Ill with fever, he decided to go with her to the 20th Maine.

But even separation from Eaton could not ensure there would be no contention where the spirited and fierce Isabella Fogg was concerned. When the well-being of her "boys" was at stake, she did not hesitate to react and did not seem to care whose political toes she stepped on. On February 26, 1863, Isabella--so ill "she ha[d] not set [sic] up scarcely any at all"-- dictated a letter (with Harriet Eaton as secretary) to Lieutenant Colonel G. W. Dyer, aide-de-camp to Governor Coburn of Maine. Dyer, like Isabella, was a native of Calais; indeed, he was the very same man who had helped raise the town's Sixth Regiment, and a man Isabella must have known fairly well:

Rooms of Maine Camp Relief Association
Stoneman's Station, near Falmouth
February 26th 1863

Mr. G.W. Dyer,
    Sir;

        Situated as we are near the encampment of the 20th Maine, and knowing that there exists a certain degree of anxiety, in your society, in regard to this Regiment and also having every opportunity for obtaining information concerning its sanitary condition, as well as thorough acquaintances with the officers in command, also, certain circumstances having come under my observation recently, which clearly indicate to me that it is my imperative duty to communicate with you in regard to the matter, although I must request to have it confidential, as far as my name is concerned. I am aware that many would say that it is no part of the duty of a lady to interfere in these matters, but, if I know my duty, I think it is to look after the interests of our sick men and when I know them to be maltreated and abused I feel it a duty to make it known, more especially as I learn there are steps being taken to give this miscreant a situation in some other of our Maine Regiments, solely for the purpose of getting rid of an Officer utterly void of all good principles.
   . . . This Officer is none other than the

Quartermaster, a more wicked, profane, cruel, unprincipled man, I think could not be found in the State of Maine. You are aware, that there have been three movements made this winter by the Army of the Potomac, first the battle of Fredericksburg, second, a reconnaissance in force, third, that last great failure to cross the river. Each time very many sick were left on the ground, and all the other Officers being needed with the Regiments, as a matter of course, this man was left in charge of the camp ground. Words would be tame to describe the abuses these poor sufferers received at his hand, the heart sickens at the thought. Poor, sick men, scarcely able to walk, were dragged from their little shelter tents, in a drenching rain, to stand guard over an old lame horse, because, forsooth, it was the private property of the surgeon, as if the loss of a horse was to be compared with the life of one of the brave sons of Maine. It was painful, truly painful, to be compelled to witness such abuse. I could name very many more, such as driving out these helpless victims to bury one of their comrades, telling them with horrid oaths, that if they were not expeditious in hustling him into the ground, he would cause a hole to be dug in which to inter them. The haste commanded was the more painful, as the spirit had just departed and the body was not yet cold. I am aware that many have censured their young, but gallant and brave Colonel [*Ames*], but this, as far as my knowledge extends, is unjust, I have never yet observed anything that would lead me to think that these charges were correct. On the

contrary he has acted on every suggestion we
have given for the comfort of his men, especially
the sick, & he has given us every facility in his
power to carry out our plans for their relief. But
this Quartermaster has never failed to tell the
men, even in my hearing, that all these outrages
were ordered by the Colonel, himself, which I
have every reason to believe was wholly untrue,
and hence the discontent there has existed in
regard to their Commanding Officer. Being well
assured that you will not deem an apology
necessary for calling your attention to these facts.

I remain very respectfully yours,
Isabella Fogg

The quartermaster was Alden Litchfield, from Rockland,
Maine, and there is independent evidence that he was every bit
as harsh and brutal as Isabella contends in this letter. And
although Isabella's letter reveals an acid "pen" (which we can
assume was well matched by her tongue), there is no doubt that
her concern was for nothing but the welfare of the soldiers in her
care. She simply was not willing to accept the suffering which
she felt--quite rightly, it appears--could have and should have
been spared the men.

Still, the position of quartermaster was perhaps a more
political one than any other in the regiment, for there was power
to be had in the ability to choose who was to make money
selling to the army, and quartermasters had a role in that
decision. Moreover, the businessmen who provided goods for
the army were quite capable of protecting their interests. In this
power struggle Alden Litchfield was the victor: he remained in
his position with the 20th Maine until the end of the war.

In March and April of 1863 Isabella was forced to her

bed in camp for five weeks by a pneumonia whose effects she had evidently been feeling since February. An excellent nurse, she was an extremely poor patient. On March 18, Eaton noted in her diary that the doctor had "called, medicines have been left, and mustard ordered on the chest." But, she added, ". . . [h]ere lays the powder, she will not take it and there is the mustard draft, she will not have it on." And two days later, on the 20th, Eaton recorded with some evident irritation that "[the doctor] has obliged [Isabella] to take a medicine that she did not choose to have and a scene has been the consequence."

During this time the army began its preparations for spring action, and Isabella, weak and ill, worried much about Hugh. About most things Harriet Eaton and Isabella Fogg did not agree, but they understood one another's mother-love perfectly. On Friday, April 17, 1863, Eaton noted in her diary:

> This morning Mrs. F[ogg] announced her intention to go to the 6th today, although she has not set up an hour at a time yet. *The reason*, Hugh returned to his Regt. *[from the hospital]*. . . . She was distressed beyond measure to think he should have returned just at this time and she determined to get him out of it. I offered to go in her stead.

At the Sixth Maine Eaton was able to convince the colonel that his regiment "needed another man to take care of their horses and [he] said that Hugh should have the place. . . ." ". . . I came back light hearted," she exulted.

Well or not, when Isabella heard--on the last day of April--that the army was on the march, she began to pack medicines and other supplies, and she directed a reluctant Eaton to do the same. The following day, May 1, Eaton noted in her diary, "The battle has commenced, we hear the sound of war

"THEY ARRIVE A FESTERING MASS. . . ."
KATHARINE WORMELEY

near at hand. . . ." So began Chancellorsville.

For days Isabella and Eaton nursed the wounded at the United States Ford "as they came pouring from the field." And later they tended those who had been taken to a house set up as hospital. There were so many wounded that the ground around this place was covered with their bodies. Isabella's mother's heart must have broken many times during the days she spent here, for Hugh's regiment, the Sixth Maine, suffered 169 men and officers wounded or killed on the battlefield at Chancellorsville. "The battle still rages," Eaton wrote on May 3, "we barely hold our own, but at Fredericksburg Sedgwick has taken the heights. The Sixth Maine has suffered severely, Major Haycock killed."

Reports from the Maine Camp Hospital Association written in the first part of 1863 provide these accounts of the nurses' work:

> Their labors at Chancellorsville are already history; the only nurses or agents on the ground with supplies when the battle opened, they received and administered to the first company of wounded sent back from the front; were shelled once from their position, but continued their heroic work until the army retreated. . . . Thus they labored for five days . . . giving nourishment, bathing wounds. . . .
>
> * * * * *
>
> . . . With their own hands they cut off the shirts all saturated with blood, from men who had been rendered helpless by wounds, washed their faces, fed them, and, in fact, did for them just what wives, mothers and sisters would have done for them had they been there.

In late May, Dr. Freeland S. Holmes wrote to Isabella concerning supplies--and gratitude:

Headquarters 6th Maine Vols.
Camp near White Oak Church
Army of the Potomac, May 27, 1863

Mrs. Fogg:
Dear Madam:
Please send by bearer the packages you spoke of. We are, I think, on the eve of another great battle. The articles I received from you before Chancellorville [*sic*] was [*sic*] the means of saving many lives on the battleground of those terrible days. You can never know how thankful I was for them.

Pardon me for saying that the friends of Maine soldiers can never realize how much they are indebted to you for such hazardous, arduous and untiring watchfulness of the wants of our men; and not only are we made the recipients of your care, but I may add the wounded and sick of the whole army. I do not hesitate to say . . . that the lives you have already been the means of saving may be counted by thousands, and I sincerely trust that those of us who may live through this conflict will not be unmindful of their obligations to you in our day of peace.

Yours, with very great respect,
F. S. Holmes
Surgeon in Charge

Isabella carried on her work at Stoneman's Station in June of 1863, where at one point she went under a flag of truce granted by General Robert E. Lee to treat the wounded. July found Eaton and Fogg at Gettysburg, arriving on the field July 4, where Isabella was relieved to find dozens of other workers ministering to the wounded. Throughout the rest of the summer and into the fall of 1863, with Hugh (after months in the hospital) now detached from his unit and driving her ambulance, Isabella moved from the scene of one battle to another: Warrenton, Culpepper, Bristoe Station, Rappahannock Station, Kelly's Ford and Mine Run.

In the early winter of 1863, trouble caught up with her. Whether it was ultimately a case of conflicting personalities, as some claim, or that she had made of Quartermaster Litchfield of the 20th Maine a fatally vindictive enemy will probably never be known. What is known is that in November of 1863 the Maine Camp Hospital Association decided, "[i]n consequence to reports prejudicial to the character and usefulness of Mrs. Fogg," to vote Isabella out of the organization and decided "for their good and the good of the cause, to dissolve their association with her." She was apparently "replaced" by Mrs. R. S. Mayhew, a native of Rockland (hometown of her nemesis, Quartermaster Litchfield), who had appeared on the field representing the Maine Camp Hospital Association shortly after the Battle of Gettysburg. After October it was no longer Fogg's, but Mayhew's signature which appeared on the blue receipts for goods and supplies from the Association.

This unwanted disassociation from an organization to which Isabella had given so much was done in spite of glowing endorsements from such men as (then) Colonel Joshua Chamberlain, the commander (after Colonel Ames) of the 20th Maine, who wrote: "I consider Mrs. Fogg to be one of the most faithful, earnest, and efficient workers in the humane cause in which she has been engaged." And a letter written in November to the Governor of Maine and signed by 32 commanding officers, chaplains, and surgeons of Maine regiments in the field expresses

> appreciation of the valuable services of Mrs. Fogg and her associates towards sick and wounded soldiers from the State of Maine . . . the welfare of our men is more promptly and effectually secured by their aid than by the ordinary Hospital and Sanitary appliances.
> We have seen these ladies in the near vicinity of the battlefields. . . . We have seen them, too, in Camp, exposing themselves to every hardship, fearing neither toil nor contagion nor inclement storm, in their patient round of duties. . . .

Isabella's struggle to remain with the Maine Camp Hospital Association was in vain, but she was not willing to leave the field--not while there was work to be done, and certainly not until Hugh's three-year enlistment with the Sixth Maine was up. After a brief return to Maine, this time to Bangor to collect new supplies, Isabella--as ever, undaunted--joined the Christian Commission, working with churches in Bangor to collect supplies for the front. The Maine State Legislature apparently retained its faith in Isabella Fogg, for in March they appropriated a substantial (for the day) sum of money ($200) to help her in her work.

In late April, Fogg was in Alexandria (across the Potomac from Washington)--where Hugh was again sick and in the hospital. This time the diagnosis was syphilis, and while this is what the record clearly states, it is possible that what Hugh Fogg suffered from was a complication of smallpox vaccination,

[37]

HOSPITAL WARD IN ALEXANDRIA

a problem rampant in 1864. That year, in the face of what it perceived as a threatened epidemic (particularly among the army), the government in Washington passed a law to the effect that any person who had not been vaccinated within the previous five years must do so or face severe penalty. The careless methods of vaccination used by many soldiers to vaccinate one another (using scabs and "rusty pins, old penknives, or whatever was handy") produced severe infection with syphilis-like symptoms, and sometimes even spread syphilis itself.

It is, of course, also possible that Hugh did indeed suffer from a syphilis contracted in the more usual way. Washington, D.C., was reported at the time to have 5,000 prostitutes, and another 2,500 were said to be in Alexandria--making one prostitute for almost every three soldiers stationed in and around the city. Opportunities existed even for soldiers in the field. An anonymous Union soldier alludes to one such opportunity in a November 9, 1866, letter to Frank Moore--who had that year published his tribute to several of the women who had served the Union as nurses. In this letter the soldier cautions Moore about a certain young woman whom Moore had included in his book. "I do not like to write," he states,

> anything that I am not willing to put my name to, but you will excuse me when you know it [is] only to give you a hint that if you intend issuing another edition of the *Women of the War*, that you had better make some inquiries about [this young woman's] character before you put her along with true hearted girls like Georgy Willets, Mary Shelton, or Maria Hall. Most any one of our old Roundhead Regt. [*100th Pennsylvania*] except the *Col.* can give you a great deal of information.

While Hugh languished in the hospital at Alexandria, the Sixth Maine spent the rest of May in the fiery Wilderness and at Spotsylvania, where more than half the regiment was lost at the Mule Shoe and almost a quarter of those remaining at the Bloody Angle. Colonel Joshua Chamberlain described the groans and cries of the wounded at the Wilderness as "a wail far and deep and wide." In the darkness, "through the murk," he saw

> dusky forms of ghostly ambulances gliding upon the far edge of the field, pausing here and there to gather up their precious freight; and the low-hovering half-covered lanterns, or blue gleam of a lighted match, held close over a brave, calm face, to know whether it were of the living or the dead.

When these wounded were brought to the hospitals set up in Fredericksburg, Isabella was there to tend them, "toiling day and night without sleep" among the men who lay "helpless upon . . . *bare, wet, bloody* floors." About what she saw after the Wilderness she later wrote, "It was indescribable in its enormous woes, a sight demanding the tears and prayers of the universe-- the awful price of a nation's existence."

In June she followed the army to Port Royal, about 25 miles below Fredericksburg and near the Sixth at Cold Harbor; then she was on to City Point on the James River, where what was left of the Sixth Maine convened in July when their original three-year term of enlistment was up and the regiment was ordered to Maine for discharge. Hugh was still confined in the hospital, this time as a convalescent patient at Emory General in Washington, but Isabella was confident enough in his eventual recovery to at last leave the field and sail north, "returning to Boston and then to Calais." In September of 1864 Isabella began working with the Ladies' Christian Commission of Bangor; she

[40]

WOUNDED MEN WITH THEIR NURSE AT HOSPITAL IN FREDERICKSBURG

was to be "sent to make reports of the work [of the Commission] in such towns and villages of Maine as she may be able to reach, to form auxiliary associations. . . ."

But if Isabella's plans also included preparing for Hugh's homecoming and looking forward to spending time in Calais with him, she was to be tragically disappointed. Many of the men of the Sixth Maine had reenlisted, and along with veterans of the Fifth and Seventh Maine Regiments and some new recruits had been consolidated into the Sixth Battalion, afterwards the First Regiment Infantry, Maine Veteran Volunteers. Among these was Hugh Fogg. After months--even years--under his mother's overly watchful eye, the slight, sickly young man was at last on his own. Recovered enough to join his new unit, he was with General Sheridan in Virginia's Shenandoah Valley.

On August 21, 1864, Hugh's unit had participated in the Battle of Charlestown; on September 17 came the fighting at Winchester; and on the 21st that at Fisher's Hill. On Wednesday, October 19, 1864, the Confederates, moving unnoticed through a heavy pre-dawn fog, began an attack on the Federals at Cedar Creek (Belle Grove), Virginia. An officer described the scene:

> Here and there were splashes of blood, and zigzag trails of blood, and bodies of men and horses. I never on any other battlefield saw so much blood as on this of Cedar Creek. The firm limestone soil would not receive it and there was no pitying summer grass to hide it.

Sometime during the fierce fighting that day, a minie ball struck Hugh in the left leg, shattering the bone and causing an immediate and severe infection. One of 3,425 Federals wounded at Cedar Creek, he was taken from the field to a hospital at Winchester where the next day his leg was amputated two inches

COMMISSION.

The United States Christian Commission, organized nearly at the outset of the present war, has, through its agents, accomplished a vast amount of labor for the physical and moral benefit of our soldiers. The demand for delegates to visit the hospitals, camps and battle-fields with their personal sympathy and ministrations, with stores for the sick and wounded, and with good reading matter, is still most urgent, and appeals to the patriotic and Christian heart for prayers and gifts.

In the number of benevolent and Christian ladies who have given their personal services to the work of consolation and help in the Hospitals of the Army, is MRS. ISABELLA FOGG, of Calais, Maine. With passes and recommendations from Generals Grant, Meade, Williams, Chamberlain, Ingalls, Prince, and other officers of the Army of the Potomac, ministering chiefly to the soldiers from our own State.

That supplies may not fail in this hour of need, she is sent to make reports of the work in such towns and villages of Maine as she may be able to reach, to form auxiliary associations, and by such means as she may deem best to promote an interest and hearty co-operation.

She is instructed to act under the general direction of the Ladies' Christian Commission of Bangor, and to report results to us.

Most earnestly do we commend her and the cause to the favor of all who love the Nation and would do somewhat in fellowship with those who seek to alleviate the hardships and temptations of the brave men who are defending the Nation's life.

MRS. G. W. PICKERING, *President.*
MRS. J. B. FOSTER, *Vice President.*
MRS. THOMPSON, *Secretary.*
MRS. GIDDINGS, *Treasurer.*

EXECUTIVE COMMITTEE:

MRS. QUIMBY,	MRS. ADAMS,	MRS. METCALF,
MRS. SHAW,	MRS. KIMBALL,	MRS. HODGKINS,
MRS. BURBANK,	MRS. WITHERS,	MRS. MERRILL,
MRS. BRADLEY,	MISS POND,	MRS. INGALLS,
MRS. PERKINS,		MRS. BRAGDEN.

BANGOR, Sept. 27th, 1864.

The undersigned are happy to assure the churches and communities of Maine that MRS. ISABELLA FOGG is in every way worthy of confidence in the blessed mission she has undertaken.

J. S. BURGESS, Pastor F. W. B. Church.
A. K. P. SMALL, Pastor 1st Baptist Church.
ENOCH POND, Theo. Seminary.
CHARLES G. PORTER, Pastor 2d Baptist Church.
EDWIN JOHNSON, Pastor Hammond St. Church, Cong.

ISABELLA'S COMMISSION

above the knee.

In Calais Isabella received word of her son's injury and quickly began to make her way back to Virginia, this time to the Shenandoah Valley. At Winchester she found to her great relief that her son had survived his traumatic surgery; from there she accompanied him to Patterson Post Hospital in Baltimore, where she stayed at his side to nurse him (as well as the other sick and wounded in his ward) until he was out of danger. But the shock of the news of Hugh's injury, the hard journey to find him, the long days of nursing, and the sleepless nights of worry exacted their price, and as soon as her son was out of danger Isabella collapsed from exhaustion.

When she recovered she decided not to return to Calais. Instead she was ready to work once more as a nurse in the field, and she offered her services again to the Christian Commission in Washington. But by this time attitudes regarding women nurses had changed, and a great number of additional volunteer nurses had come to Washington. Because of this and the fact that large numbers of soldiers were being discharged from the army during the same period, the great need for nurses had disappeared in the eastern theater. However, a need still existed in the western part of the country, and so Isabella was assigned to duty aboard the hospital boat *Jacob Strader*, which was then operating on the Ohio River out of Louisville, Kentucky. It was aboard the *Jacob Strader* in January of 1865, while taking a glass of wine to a dying soldier "in the dusk of evening," that Isabella stumbled on deck and fell through a hatchway, very seriously injuring her spine. She was "completely helpless for upwards of two years, during which time . . . she [was] confined to her bed during the whole of this period."

Isabella Fogg had done enough nursing to realize how seriously hurt she was, to know that she would be crippled--perhaps for life. And now that she would no longer be able to care for Hugh once he left the hospital, her first concern was for

AN AMPUTATION

"Tables . . . had been erected upon which screaming victims were having legs and arms cut off. . . . The surgeons and their assistants . . . bespattered with blood, stood around, some holding the poor fellows, while others, armed with long, bloody knives and saws, cut and sawed away with frightful rapidity. . . ."

—FROM *Tenting Tonight*

his welfare. In a letter written only days after her accident and which her condition obviously required that someone else write for her, she dictated a request to the medical director in charge of the Pennsylvania military hospitals stating her wish that Hugh be transferred to one of the hospitals in Philadelphia, where he might be educated or trained to make a living. "I am earnestly desirous," she wrote,

> that he should be admitted to Christian Street hospital in order that he may be fitted to gain his own livelihood hereafter. . . . Nothing but necessity, and an earnest desire to see my maimed and suffering child rendered competent to sustain himself comfortably through life, would prompt me to call attention to this case.

In her argument for this transfer, Isabella cites Hugh's youth (even exaggerating it by two years) at the time of his enlistment, his long service, and her widowhood. But she does not mention a word of her own disability.

She persuaded the medical director, and in time Hugh was transferred to the hospital in Philadelphia which Isabella had named as her first choice for him. For the following two years, Isabella herself remained a bedridden-patient, first in St. Luke's Hospital at Cincinnati, Ohio, and later in the Good Samaritan Hospital in the same city. ". . . I was entirely confined to my bed," she later wrote, "and dependent on friends to conduct my correspondence." Eventually her disability was taken notice of, and through the intercession of influential friends who knew of her work (such as General Chamberlain, who wrote that he hoped "the kindness she has shown . . . may be returned to her as a matter of justice") Isabella was granted a pension of eight dollars a month by a special act of congress signed on April 17, 1866, "in consideration of injuries received while in discharge of

GENERAL J. L. CHAMBERLAIN

". . . [T]hat the kindness she has shown in charity may be returned to her as a matter of justice."

—MAJOR GEN. J. L. CHAMBERLAIN
Petition for Isabella Fogg

meritorious service." She was the only woman of the Civil War granted a governmental pension for wartime injuries.

This pension, however, proved inadequate, leaving Isabella without means or ability to support herself. In May of 1866 a friend in Cincinnati commented that Isabella's situation was one of "extreme helplessness & poverty," adding that "[s]he is supported by the gifts of strangers in [the] city hospital."

From her bed Isabella tried her hand at composing poetry. "During my sufferings," she confided to a correspondent that same year, "I have written a few poems, one on the Battle of Fredericksburg, another on Andersonville Prison, and some other short pieces. . . . As the spinal injury I have received will in all probability make me a cripple for life, it is important that I be able to do something for my future support." Apparently she did not receive much encouragement for these literary efforts, or perhaps the increase of her pension to $20.00 per month in 1867 made them unnecessary, for her poems were--as far as we know--never published. The former seems the more likely, since in late 1870, Isabella--released from the hospital and living in Quincy, Illinois--attempted to have her pension increased to $50.00 per month, "having tried and failed to obtain any employment at the Govt. bureaus at Washington," and being often "prostrated by severe illness caused by [her] former injuries."

Her friends and past associates from Maine provided Isabella an abundance of endorsements for her petitions. Unfortunately, Dr. Freeland S. Holmes, who, in May of 1863, had expressed his wish that Isabella would not be forgotten "in our day of peace," did not survive the war, but such men as General O. O. Howard, Colonel C. D. Gilmore, and General Joshua Chamberlain again offered their support. They noted that "her services to the sick and wounded were constant and invaluable," and that she had "serv[ed] on twenty nine battle grounds, and [been] exposed to the fire of the enemy eight times."

In March of 1871 Isabella's pension was increased, though to $30.00 and not $50.00 per month; at the same time she at last obtained work in the Pension Office in Washington, D.C. She was still very frail, and so lame she was forced to use a crutch--the act of simply getting to her work in the city must have been extrememly trying for her.

Isabella never returned to Calais, but spent her last years in hospitals in Ohio and Illinois, and in private homes in Quincy, Illinois, in Portland and finally in Washington, where, near the familiar scenes of the Civil War that had consumed so much of her life and health, she died on December 22, 1873. Her body was taken to Maine and buried in South Portland, in Forest City Cemetery, where her simple granite headstone states her name and dates and, as epitaph, only the word *MOTHER*.

Hugh had been discharged from both the army and the hospital in Chester, Pennsylvania, on June 8, 1865. He gave his address on his final papers as Calais, Maine, and upon release immediately returned to Maine, where, on July 2 of the same year, he married a friend's sister, the 19-year-old Serapta Ann Fuller of Portland. In 1868 he and Serapta (they were and remained childless) moved to Ft. Leavenworth, Kansas, where Hugh was Superintendent of the National Cemetery until 1879, when he was ordered to change climate because of his failing health. He went then to be Superintendent of Cave Hill National Cemetery in Louisville, Kentucky, where he died of consumption (tuberculosis) on January 1, 1880. He is buried at Cave Hill. Hugh Fogg was almost 37 years old when he died, the age his mother had been that long-ago spring of a different world when the two of them had first sailed from Calais for the fields of war.

Neither Isabella nor Hugh Fogg lived a long life, but both lived long enough to take part in the most important event of their time. They also lived to see, as Isabella herself is said to have stated, "the triumph of the right, and the dawn of peace, and the days when the patriot, no longer languishing in camp nor agonizing on the field, will not suffer for what woman, in her tenderness, can do for him. . . ."

CIVIL WAR MONUMENT IN CALAIS, MAINE

CHAPTER III

SARAH SERVED
The Civil War Story of
SARAH SMITH SAMPSON

One there is sleeping in yonder low tomb,
Worthy the brightest of flowers that bloom. . . .
Bravely she stood by the sufferer's side,
Checking the pain and the life-bearing tide;
Fighting the swift-sweeping phantom of Death,
Easing the dying man's fluttering breath;
Then, when the strife that had nerved her was o'er,
Calmly she went to where wars are no more.
Voices have blessed her now silent and dumb;
Voices will bless her in long years to come.
Cover her over--yes, cover her over--
Blessings, like angels, around her should hover;
Cherish the name of that sister of ours,
And cover her over with beautiful flowers.
                                    --WILL CARLETON

In a far corner of Arlington National Cemetery, among large and small monuments and near one of those fields of white stone by which we truly count the cost of war, is the grave of a woman named Sarah Smith Sampson. She was the wife of a Civil War soldier and the friend of great generals, but those who know her story understand well that Sarah Sampson has earned her own place in this hallowed ground.

Arlington Cemetery, near Washington, D.C., is some six

[51]

hundred miles from Bath, Maine, where Sarah was born sometime in the mid-1830's, the vivacious, charming, and very determined daughter of Joseph and Lucy Smith. Other than the fact she had a brother, Lewis, and a sister, Mary, little is known of her years growing up in Bath. We can assume that from a young age she was exposed to people and ideas from all parts of the eastern seaboard, for at the time Sarah lived in Bath the town was a busy seaport whose cultural and business ties to the ports of the American South were stronger than those to many of the cities and villages in the rest of New England.

In 1855 Sarah--"probably a young woman of 20"--married Charles A. L. Sampson, a handsome and skilled ship's carver who had been born in Boston (in 1825), but who was at the time of his marriage employed in Bath, where his figureheads graced some of the finest seagoing vessels. Until 1861 both Charles and Sarah were hidden in the deep shadows of the history of ordinary people. But when the Civil War broke out, Charles became Captain of Company D of the Third Maine Regiment of Volunteers, whose Colonel was Oliver Otis Howard, and Sarah attached herself to this regiment as a nurse. Her reason for going to the war, she later said, was "because my husband was called to the front, and I wanted to go with him"; and she promised herself to care for the soldiers of the regiment "while the war should continue."

On the morning of June 5, 1861, Sarah left the Maine state capital of Augusta with the Third Maine for the army "base" at Washington. She went with the "recommendation" of the Adjutant General of Maine, General John L. Hodsdon, and "under the protection" of the commander of the Third Maine, (then) Colonel O. O. Howard. In her possession was a letter of introduction from Dr. Alonzo Garcelon, Surgeon General of Maine and one of the men of her acquaintance who today might be called "mentors," men of influence on whom it was Sarah's habit to turn, when necessary, a powerful and usually successful

GENERAL OLIVER OTIS HOWARD

combination of charm and determination. From Washington several days later (June 14, 1861) Sarah wrote to Dr. Garcelon in Maine:

> Our journey from Augusta to Washington was to me truly delightful. Nothing occurred "en route" that might have disturbed or annoyed the most sensitive--I traveled as you left me in the car with the "Staff" and every object of interest was pointed out to me in the most agreeable manner. Our Col. and his *brother* . . . were very friendly to me; and I felt when at 8 o'clock Friday evening I arrived at "Willards Hotel" and reviewed the past three days, that I had entered upon my new life under really favorable auspices.

The next morning, Saturday the 9th, Sarah, with her letter of introduction from Dr. Garcelon in hand, went to call on Dorthea Dix, who was very soon to be in charge of recruiting, approving, and assigning women nurses for the army, and who was at the time in charge of the general hospital in Washington. Some of the Third Maine's sick soldiers had been denied entrance to the general hospital, and Sarah sought help from Dix. Finding that "the lady was out," Sarah struck up a conversation with Dix's housekeeper, a native of Maine, and, she wrote to Dr. Garcelon, "from her . . . learned many items." It was, she said angrily, "through her that our sick soldiers (seven in number) were *not* admitted to the *Gen. Hospital* the evening of our arrival in Washington."

The housekeeper told Sarah that Dix was "*noble, genuine,* and *patriotic,* but that she had really now taken more than she was able to get through with." And in addition "it was dangerous conflicting with [Dix's] idea." In the end Sarah decided that she was "glad *now*" that the sick soldiers had not been admitted to the hospital: ". . . others might serve the sick, but they must be under *her control.* . . ." Not only was it better not to involve the care of the regiment's sick with Dorthea Dix, but more could be done for the sick and wounded outside of any regulations: this latter conclusion on Sarah Sampson's part, it should be noted, was to become her guiding principle for the rest of the war.

Still, influenced by common prewar political opinion which placed allegiance to and identification with one's home state before national interests, Sarah's specific plans required the involvement of the people of her native state. "We should have a *Maine Gen.* Hospital," she wrote,

> and "female *nurses* [from Maine] are much more efficient than men. Our surgeon thinks it exceedingly *necessary* that we should be provided with such. . . . [O]ur own people at *home* can easily see the advantages we should receive in keeping our Maine sick by ourselves. . . . [It] would save many a Mother's and Sister's tears to feel their dear ones more tenderly cared for, by Mother and sisters from our own state.

The Monday after her conversation with Dix's housekeeper--and three days after her arrival in Washington--Sarah made her way to Meridian Hill, where the Second, Third, Fourth, and Fifth Maine were all camped together. Here was "a large old brick building" being used as a hospital, where those sick soldiers who had been refused by Dix were being cared for by Dr. Gideon S. Palmer, the (then) surgeon of the Third Maine. Sarah offered her services, which were apparently very much needed and welcomed. "It is *quite sickly* among us," she reported to Dr. Garcelon, "[as] there are twenty cases of Camp dysentery this morning, and we had twenty cases of mumps."

From this point on, Sarah moved from camp to camp with the regimental "hospital"--which, as she had hoped, was indeed supplied and furnished by the people of Maine.

One man who quickly became one of Sarah's on-scene mentors was the regimental commander, Colonel Howard, with whom Sarah had a friendly personal relationship which quickly grew into a deep mutual respect. Sarah nursed Howard when he fell ill, and in late June he wrote home to his wife Lizzie that "Mrs. Sampson is one of the best women for the sick room I ever saw. . . ." And in his autobiography, he credited the saving of his life in part to ". . . the care given [him] by the wife of Captain Sampson."

But Sarah's interest in the regiment was not limited to its commander and other officers. She was devoted to all of the soldiers of the Third Maine. She wrote to the families of the privates lying in the hospitals to tell them about the condition of their loved ones, and she wrote to the families of the dead about the funerals, which she attended whenever possible, including in her letters whatever keepsakes she could. "I wrote a long letter to his wife," she reported about one soldier, "at the time of his death . . . and again after the funeral[,] sending her a lock of hair and some pressed rose-leaves that had lain on his bosom. I have since visited his grave. . . ."

From the first, she loved her work. ". . . I am perfectly well," she wrote after her first week with the regiment, "and never happier in my life than now. . . ." Until First Bull Run (First Manassas) on July 21 of 1861, she visited the hospital (which in truth was any place the sick were, whether a large building or simply a clearing in the woods) daily, spending almost every waking hour with the patients. When the Third Maine left camp to take part in the battle of First Bull Run, Sarah stayed behind to look after the sick. It was only when the regiment moved with the rest of the army from Manassas to Alexandria--across the river from the old camp at Meridian Hill--

that Sarah left the camp hospital. Then she too went to Alexandria, to care for the men who had been wounded at Bull Run, as well as those who had been "broken down by the march." It was here, on the 23rd of July, that Sarah first met President Lincoln. She had been up all night, as she later told it,

with the wounded soldiers, on the third floor of a warehouse. In the morning Edward Donnell of Bath came up and told me that Mr. Lincoln was down in the street.

I ran down and saw a carriage near the door. Going up to it, I said to the gentleman I saw inside, "Are you Mr. Lincoln?" "No, my name is Seward," he told me. "I want to see the President," I said. "I came down three flights of stairs on purpose to see him." "He is here," said Mr. Seward, smiling. "I will get out and you can take my place in the carriage." So he got out and I jumped in, [by the] side of Mr. Lincoln. He looked just like the pictures. . . . A kindly, rugged face, a strong, friendly face, that one could always trust. . . .

. . . We talked a long time, and he showed the keenest interest and sympathy in my work. . . . He was . . . a splendid man, the best man I ever saw on earth. . . .

During the winter of 1861-1862 the army stayed in camp and Sarah stayed with it, as ever tending to the sick and the wounded. Sometimes she was joined by other women from Maine; at other times she was the only female nurse.

When spring arrived and the army began to move forward, to her deep disappointment Sarah was left behind.

Washington had become a military city, and Virginia, across the river, was enemy territory. Passes were required into Virginia, as they were required in order to pass through any of the Union lines, and passes were particularly difficult to obtain without connections. Sarah was not connected, not to the army, or the Sanitary Commission, or the Christian Commission, or even to one of the newly formed state relief societies. At last, however, after the fighting at Williamsburg (which took place on May 5, 1862), she managed to receive from Senator Morrill "a pass and transportation for [her] supplies to the army for three months," and she eagerly moved forward. From this point until the end of the war, Sarah was somehow able to have this pass renewed every three months, making it possible for her to be just where she wanted to be, with the sick and wounded of Maine--doing exactly what she wanted to be doing, spending her days and nights at the bedsides of ill and dying soldiers. "My sick soldiers were scattered everywhere," she wrote, "and everywhere I would seek for them."

Sarah was at White House Landing on June 2, 1862, just after Fair Oaks when (now) General Howard and his brother were brought in wounded, "the former with his right arm amputated, and the latter with a severe flesh wound in the thigh." Like the rest of the Union army, the Third Maine suffered many casualties at Fair Oaks. "Such suffering and confusion I never before witnessed," Sarah said. She "procured [her] food from the [hospital] stewards and rested wherever [she] might be overcome with sleep," often watching by the bed of a patient.

On June 25, 1862, the first day of what came to be called the Seven Days' Battle, Sarah and other female nurses from Maine, "hearing that Hooker's Division was engaged . . . packed [their] wagons and hurried to the field," where all day they "worked among and for [the wounded], preparing drinks, dressing wounds. . . ."

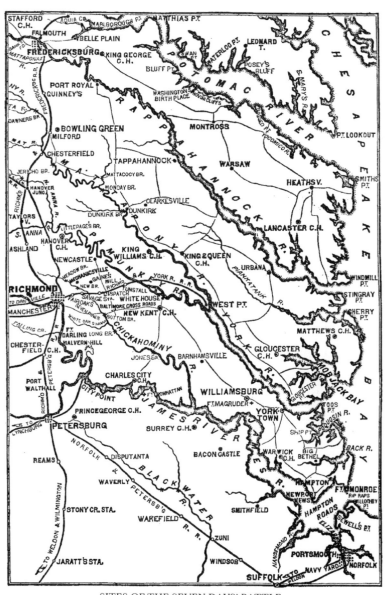

SITES OF THE SEVEN DAYS' BATTLE

From White House Landing Sarah and the other nurses went to Yorktown, and on July 1, 1862, they traveled from there by hospital steamer to meet the massive army retreating from Malvern Hill to Harrison's Landing on the James River, where many wounded Maine soldiers were expected. "The estimated four thousand ambulances and wagons arrived throughout the day and night bearing wounded men and supplies. That evening the four hundred supply ships and transports began arriving. . . ." Sarah wrote that she and her associates

> reached there at night, and early the next morning the wounded were brought to us in small boats, as we were anchored in the stream, no wharves yet having been built. The groaning of the poor fellows, as they were lifted from one boat to another, was heart-rending.

Another nurse described what life was like among the wounded aboard the hospital transports such as the one Sarah then served on. "Imagine," she said, "a great . . . steamer filled on every deck--every berth and every square inch of room covered with wounded men":

> Men in every condition of horror, shattered and shrieking, were being brought in on stretchers borne by "contrabands," who dumped them anywhere, banged the stretchers against pillars and posts, and walked over the men without compassion. . . . Men shattered in the thigh, and even cases of amputation, were shoved into top berths without thought or mercy. . . .
> . . . All we could do at first was to try to calm the confusion, to stop some agony. . . .

HOSPITAL TRANSPORT FOR SICK AND WOUNDED

The worst of the sad results of the rushed evacuation to Harrison's Landing in the first days of July of 1862 was that many wounded were left behind. The disastrous night retreat of the army turned out to be "one of the most demoralizing" events of the war for the Federals. Officers and men alike spoke bitterly about the "'indelible disgrace' of a victorious army leaving its wounded on the field. . . ." Union General Philip Kearny asserted that the order for the march to the landing was "prompted by cowardice or treason" on the part of the army's commander, General George McClellan. And speaking of the entire horrible scene, a New York doctor said it was "enough to melt the heart of the stoutest." (Soon after, a new medical director, Dr. Jonathan Letterman, was appointed to reorganize the medical department of the military, to set up a plan for effective field hospitals and an efficient ambulance system.)

July was a particularly unsettling time for Sarah: the movements of the army had thus far been unsuccessful--even their "victory" at Malvern Hill had resulted in the double tragedy of the wounded being abandoned and those men able to move being subjected to an exhausting march. Added to this, Sarah's personal life had also become unsettled. She loved her work in the field; in fact, her early letters leave the distinct impression of a soul unfettered--"*I have never been happier in my life. . . .*" The Civil War, so tragic and disastrous for so very many, had given Sarah the opportunity to break out of the bounds of her former life--the life of a wife and member of a tightly controlled community--and do what she seems to have been born for.

But Sarah's husband Charles, though promoted from captain to lieutenant colonel (skipping the rank of major) in the Third Maine and in line for further promotion, was unable to find his rightful place in the great conflict. On July 7, 1862, he resigned his commission--under force. He had been ill for some time with a fever whose effects he was to feel for the rest of his shortened life, but poor health does not seem to have been the reason Charles was encouraged to leave the army; the cause was more likely Charles' reaction to the flawed military policy of the leaders of the Union Army which had resulted in such terrible losses and ill-planned movements as he had witnessed since the summer of 1861. Charles' military file at the National Archives notes his "arrest" in June, indicating that it was for his "conduct . . . on the night of [June] 25th. . . ."--at the end of that first calamitous day of the Seven Days' Battle.

With Sarah, Charles Sampson sailed for home in Maine. "He has lost none of his *patriotism*," Sarah explained in a letter to General Hodsdon, the Adjutant General of Maine, "though I think his confidence in some of the commanders somewhat shaken *at least*." "It is with great reluctance," she added,

> that I leave at a time when my services are so much, *never so much* needed . . . but I feel my *first* duty is to my husband, who would not on any account permit me to remain even were I disposed to.

Sarah wanted desperately to return to the hospitals in the South, and to her work there. And although she expressed the hope that after some rest Charles would again "be able to offer his services to his country" and that she would be able to go with him, a later letter from Sarah to General Hodsdon, this one from her home in Bath in August of 1862, indicates that she knew her return would depend entirely on her own devices. "I am so anxious to learn if I am to be successful in my endeavor for our sick in the Army," she wrote. Pleading further she added, "I am not easily discouraged but just now, to save time, I need all the help I can get. . . ."

In its entirety Sarah's letter is in essence a long appeal for help so that she might return to service with the army, either in company with someone else, or "alone as before." She stated

[63]

her position clearly: "Our poor boys must not suffer for what is their due--they *shall* not--as far as I am able to relieve them." And in a postscript she hinted at a deep frustration: "I am hoping to be able to get away by another week; I feel that every day that is spent here [in Bath] is wasted."

She seems to have been disappointed in the general's reply (if there was a reply), for not only the next week but the next month found her still home; by then she apparently had decided to turn to another possible source of aid, the "Ladies of Bath." In a September 2, 1862, letter they appealed, on their behalf and Sarah's, to the governor of Maine. "That we may [send supplies] with confidence," they wrote,

> someone in whom we can trust should be on the ground, to receive & appropriate such Contributions. Feeling satisfied that Mrs. Sampson has peculiar natural qualifications for this ministry of mercy, and that she has been very useful there in months past, & also that the experience thus gained is of immeasurable value, we know of no woman whom we could more cheerfully make our almoner in this enterprise.
>
> We do therefore most earnestly petition your Excellency, to grant her a pass to her former field of labor, in the immediate vicinity of the M[ain]e Regiments. And while the groans of suffering are borne to us on every breeze from the battlefields of Virginia, we feel constrained to add the earnest request that your Excellency will give to our petition the earliest attention in your power.

In the end Sarah's goal was, somehow, accomplished, and by October--with the support of the Ladies' Aid of Bath, but still not connected officially to any organization--she was at last where she longed to be, at the seat of war ready to work once again. "I proceeded to Washington," she wrote, "feeling sure I was in the path of duty, and that a kind Providence would guide me."

In Washington she renewed a previously brief acquaintance with Mr. and Mrs. George W. Hall, at the time residents of Washington, but formerly of Maine. Mrs. Hall was active in hospital work, and Sarah began accompanying her on daily visits to the various hospitals in the city, dispensing the supplies sent to her by the Ladies' Aid Society of Bath. Soon Sarah had an appointment (with $40.00 per month pay) to the Maine Soldiers' Relief Association, an organization made up of citizens of Maine residing in Washington. Now her official duties were to visit the military hospitals in and near Washington to "ascertain the name, rank, regiment, company, residence and wants of each patient, and, so far as possible, supply the want from the stores of the Association." In this position Sarah had a two-horse ambulance and a driver detailed to carry her and her supplies around the city.

Sarah carried on this work throughout the fall of 1862, until December when the large numbers of severely wounded from the Battle of Fredericksburg drew her southward from Washington to Falmouth--directly across the river from Fredericksburg--where she visited the sick and wounded of the Third, Fourth, and Seventeenth Maine Regiments. She worked among the wounded of Fredericksburg until Sunday, February 8, 1863, leaving then with several extremely ill soldiers from Maine who had been discharged and whom she was determined to send on home to their native state.

Through March, April, and into May of 1863--when the wounded from Chancellorsville were brought to Washington--Sarah continued her work in the hospitals in and near Washington. In July came Gettysburg, causing Sarah and Mrs.

[65]

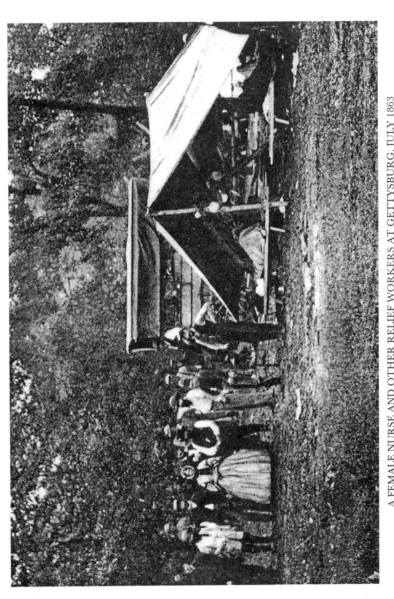

A FEMALE NURSE AND OTHER RELIEF WORKERS AT GETTYSBURG, JULY 1863

"It was hard, exhausting work, sometimes discouraging, and always sad."

—FROM *Hospital Life in the Army of the Potomac*

R. S. Mayhew of the Maine Camp and Hospital Association to hurry to the battlefield in Pennsylvania, "taking . . . all the supplies that could be spared. . . ." From Sarah's own journal is the following account of her work there, written three weeks after the battle:

> Morning of Friday, July 24th. But two stretchers (with deceased soldiers) appear outside the hospital tents this morning. Yesterday there were five, and three others died during the day. We made the rounds of the hospital (1st Div., 3[r]d Corps) to ascertain the condition of the patients, and return to our quarters; Mrs. M[ayhew] to make tea and chocolate for the patients (in spirit lamps purchased with money from the ladies of Auburn[, Maine]), and I to make fly screens for Sergt. Allen and Allen Sprague of 3[r]d Maine, both very low with wounds. Mrs. S. of Gettysburg kept her promise in sending me a pair of shears, and I pass two hours with the patients, cutting hair, and in washing and making them comfortable. Return to quarters and find Mrs. Mayhew has opened our last barrel of supplies, hoping to find some sheets; finding none she was sewing handkerchiefs together for a covering for one. A messenger comes from 1st Corps Hospital for Jno. F. Chase of 5th Battery, who is wounded and desires to see some one from Maine. We go together and find he has lost one eye, has one arm amputated, and is quite severely wounded in the breast. We give him and others the goodies we have brought along, take items to write his mother at Togus Springs, and leave with a promise to come again

soon. Returning to quarters, find ambulance ready to take us to the city for stores from Christian Commission; return from there, and 10 o'clock finds us on the ground of our tent (no floor, no table but barrel heads), making egg-nog for which the nurses are waiting. Go into the hospitals ourselves to see some of the patients; return at midnight.

Sarah did not leave Gettysburg until mid-August of 1863; by that time most of the Maine wounded had been moved to hospitals in Baltimore and places in Pennsylvania, and so she was able to return to her work in the hospitals in Washington. Here she stayed until the Battle of the Wilderness in early May of 1864, at which time she and Mrs. Mayhew went into Fredericksburg where hospitals to take care of the casualties from that battle had been established:

All along the road we met the wounded going to Belle Plain, and our wagon being one of a train of seventy-five, we were frequently stopped by some stubborn mule or broken wheel. At such times, the soldiers would come to the wagon and ask for something to eat, having had nothing for one, two or three days. They told us doleful stories of the wounded that were being brought into Fredericksburg, and assured us "the boys would be glad to see us. . . ."

[In Fredericksburg] our supplies came up slowly at first, and we could only relieve the suffering by dressing wounds. Many were sinking for want of care, their wounds not having been dressed since they left the field hospital. Many, too, were without shelter even, and [had been] allowed to cry all night long for water.

Something of Sarah's work and methods during this time can be learned from the small diary of Rebecca Usher, another young woman from Maine who had come to nurse the soldiers of the army. One story which Rebecca records tells of a young soldier whose leg was to be amputated and Sarah's interference in the case. The boy knew Dr. Garcelon personally and told Sarah that he wanted Garcelon to perform the surgery, which was scheduled to be done by another doctor, the "Surgeon in Charge." When Sarah approached this surgeon with the boy's request that Dr. Garcelon operate on him, the surgeon not only refused to allow it, he also grilled Sarah about the boy--his name and regiment; and about Sarah--her work, her authority, and her intentions. Sarah's brief and unresponsive answer to his questions was simply, "That's of no consequence, sir."

The morning of the surgery, before the surgeon was even awake, Sarah managed to have Dr. Garcelon amputate the boy's leg, and before the good surgeon was up and about and drinking his coffee, the "stump [was] dressed and [the boy] made comfortable."

"Another time," Rebecca wrote,

> there were a number of men that [Mrs. Sampson] wanted to send home, but the surgeon had no power to send them further than Alexandria. She went with them & when they arrived at Alex[andria] she sent for the surgeon & told him she wanted an order to take these men to Washington. He said he had no power to send them. But said she, "Sir, these men are dying, & if you do let them go on, they may live to see their friends." He said he knew it was a hard case, but he could not help it; it was against

his orders. "Now," said she, "Dr., you just let me go on with these men. I know the Surgeon General & as soon as I get to Washington, I will go to him & tell him that it is all my fault, that you could not help it; that I brought the men away in spite of you." She carried her point.

The Surgeon General, Rebecca added, was "astounded at her audacity & told her she must never do such a thing again."

But, of course, she did--as, for example, the time she needed a stretcher to carry a wounded man and finding none anywhere, "rushed into the General's tent, seized his [cot frame], tipped his bed[ding] from it" and thus carried away the needed stretcher. "A very remarkable woman she must be," concluded Rebecca, "as she always carries her point in spite of red tape."

On May 28, 1864, Sarah traveled by steamer to White House Landing, where the wounded from Cold Harbor were being brought in large numbers

at all times of the day and night, much faster than shelter could be provided for them; so that we dressed wounds and in other ways cared for them on the field. . . . Here too on their way home I saw the little remnant of the 3rd Maine, whose numbers had been so depleted during their three years of service. . . . It had been my intention to have returned to Maine with this regiment, but now I could not leave. . . .

From White House Landing Sarah went to City Point, in company with the Medical Department of the Army which was moving there to care for the thousands of men who were streaming in from before Petersburg, suffering not only from their wounds but also from the intense heat and a lack of safe

AMBULANCE TRAIN NEAR CITY POINT

"Will you tell me where the friends of F. Grant [of] Co. I, 32nd Maine may be found? He died in an ambulance on the way to City Point and was identified only by a stencil-plate found in his pocket. . . ."

—SARAH SAMPSON to Adjutant General of Maine

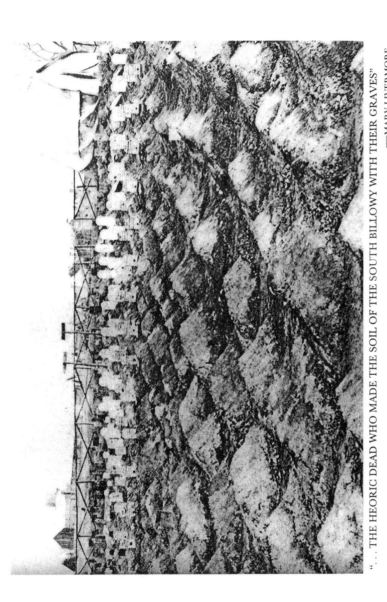

"... THE HEORIC DEAD WHO MADE THE SOIL OF THE SOUTH BILLOWY WITH THEIR GRAVES"

—MARY LIVERMORE

"... [T]he mortality among those seriously wounded, who had been brought in wagons long distances, over a rough country, was very great...."

—SARAH SAMPSON

water. Here she found "nearly seven hundred of the 1st Maine Heavy Artillery" lying in one hospital. On July 4, 1864, Sarah returned to Washington to begin a long period of work arranging for discharges and furloughs for Maine soldiers whose wounds or illnesses were such that they could not return to the field, and seeing to the many and varied needs of those who remained behind. Letters kept by the Maine Historical Society in Portland, Maine, attest to her dedication to Maine soldiers--and theirs to her. Many are requests for help from family members looking for a particular soldier or inquiring after his condition. Others are requests from the soldiers themselves. While significantly more concise than most, the content of the following letter to Sarah from a patient in Ward 26 of the Harewood Hospital typifies the basic content of most:

June 8,1864

Dear Friend;
     I want you to come hier i am wounded very bad I want to see you on particular business.

In July of 1864 Sarah wrote to General Hodsdon regarding an anticipated trip to Maine, which she had arranged in order to transport wounded and sick soldiers home where a "*change of climate* might cure [them] tho' nothing else would." "My patients," she wrote, "are delighted with the idea, and I am wild over it, as if *I* go some of the *fractures* may be taken along. My only fear is, I may not be permitted to return *if I go*." Although willing to return to Maine because doing so might benefit her patients, Sarah clearly understood she might be running a certain risk. "Please tell me *when*," she wrote in closing, "you will be ready for us, though it may be somewhat dangerous for me to go as regards my returning."
    In September of 1864 Sarah and her patients finally

sailed for home. In Bath she very soon fell ill with a severe case of malarial fever which in itself prohibited her return to Washington for several weeks. Recovering at last and ready to take up her work in the hospitals where the wounded and sick Maine soldiers lay, as expected Sarah again faced Charles' disapproval of her work in the Civil War. And as before she sought help from General Hodsdon. In December of 1864 she confided to him:

> I have been very ill since I came home, but am now rapidly recovering, and anxious to return to W[ashington]. . . .
> Mr. S[ampson] will not listen to my going back again, but I cannot think of remaining here in idleness when there is so much to be done for suffering humanity. Can you devise any means of reconciliation?

A "reconciliation" of some sort seems to have indeed been effected, for soon after Sarah was able to return to Washington and to her "boys," the soldiers in need of care. "Still under the auspices of the Maine Soldiers' Relief Association," she arrived in Washington in February of 1865, and she remained there working in the hospitals in and around the city until what turned out to be the last movements of the Union Army in the East, the battles before Petersburg and Richmond. "An order having been issued" that "a large number of surgeons. . . report without delay" to Burkeville Station, Sarah and Mrs. Mayhew boarded the first train to that place, where they were the first female nurses to arrive. "[We] found wounded being gathered from all parts of the country," Sarah reported, ". . . and the mortality among those seriously wounded, who had been brought in wagons long distances, over a rough country, was very great. . . ." Rebecca Usher, who arrived a few days later, described the conditions at Burkeville Station in a letter home:

> It is estimated that there are ten thousand patients in the hospitals here, and our Maine regiments have suffered severely. . . . Eleven hundred badly wounded were brought in on one day. In the evening the wards are dismal enough--long and narrow, without floors, dimly lighted with lanterns, and resounding with the groans of the sick and dying.

At Burkeville Station Sarah and the others were awakened in the middle of the night by someone from the Christian Commission who had come to tell them that President Lincoln had been shot. "The entire camp was wide awake," Sarah remembered later, "for the news spread like wildfire through the wards, and the patients, for a time, forgot their suffering, in the great loss of the country."

At one point someone came to the women and told them that help was desperately needed at the front where "the ground was covered" with wounded men--"the worst sight you ever saw." The nurses decided that from then on one of them would work at the front: Sarah was the first to volunteer for this duty.

Sarah did not leave Burkeville Station until after the surrender of the Confederate army in April of 1865. Then all the Union wounded were transferred to general hospitals in Washington, where Sarah joined them, "distributing supplies, securing discharges and transfers" throughout the summer of 1865. Her employment with the Maine Soldiers' Relief Association terminated in mid-August of that year, but she stayed on in Washington, feeling (in her own words) "pledged as strongly to those who suffered in striking the last blow to the

[75]

HOSPITAL IN WASHINGTON, D. C., DURING THE CIVIL WAR

rebellion, as the first, and would not leave them while they required . . . care." In those days before common knowledge of antiseptics and antibiotics, wounds often healed excruciatingly slowly, so it was October of 1865 before Sarah at long last felt free to leave Washington and return to Maine. On Friday, October 6, Sarah--"with the only remaining five wounded soldiers in hospitals . . . from our state"--boarded the hospital car of a train which reached Augusta, Maine, the following Monday (October 9, 1865). There she left them, her last patients, safely in the hospital before going home to Bath.

The Civil War had been over for six months by the time Sarah and that last little band of soldiers left the train at the station in Augusta on an evening in October of 1865, and life in Maine was returning to its more ordinary routines. Men wearing proud remnants of faded blue uniforms were taking up farming and business again, attempting as old soldiers do to put what cannot be forgotten as much out of the way of life as possible. But for Sarah Sampson, there would be no putting away her pledge to care for the men of Maine; even though the war was at last over, she could not stop serving. For months after her return to Maine she spent long hours at her desk writing letters on behalf of veterans and their families, working to help the men gain pensions, their families to locate battlefield graves, their orphaned children to find support and education. During this time she was vitally important in the founding of the Bath Military and Naval Orphan Asylum, whose purpose was to care for and educate at no charge the orphans and "half orphans" of any Union officer or enlisted man who had served from the state of Maine in the Civil War. Sarah herself adopted at least one little girl, whom she named Beatrice; she had another daughter whom she named after her own sister Mary.

On January 1, 1881, Sarah's husband Charles died without ever having, "for patriotic reasons," applied for a pension. Two years later, after unsuccessfully trying to find support in Maine, Sarah moved to Washington D.C., where she found work in the Pension Office. She was described in her later years as "sweet-faced" and "gracious," with "that serenity of manner that has rendered her specially fitted to the trials and tragedies of army nursing." Not surprisingly, she became a popular and important figure in the New England colony in Washington.

In February 1885, by a special act of Congress, Sarah was placed on the pension roll as "an army nurse, widow of Lieutenant-Colonel Charles A. L. Sampson . . . at the rate of twenty-five dollars per month"; this pension, along with her salary, allowed her and her "little family" to live fairly comfortably in the city.

Until the end of her life, Sarah Sampson remained committed to the concerns of the Third Maine Regiment, returning to Maine almost every summer in order to be a "quiet, constant attendant" at the annual reunion of the Third Maine Regiment Association; she even served as the organization's president. The men of the regiment, as they always had, adored her--she was referred to in the Maine newspapers as "the Florence Nightingale of Maine" and the "idol" of the soldiers. In May of 1900 she wrote to General Joshua Chamberlain, with whom she had formed one of her "mentor" relationships:

> I see you are to be in Bath Memorial day. I wish I were to be there to listen to your voice and words and to drop my flowers and tears on the graves of my loved ones and comrades. I *ought* to be there all the time! It was *cruel* that I was compelled to leave my dear old home for the support of my family. Mean

[78]

politicians did that. . . . I shall always feel that I deserved more consideration from my state--but most of those who appreciated my work have gone and . . . *we'll* soon follow.

In another letter to Chamberlain, this one written in November of the same year, Sarah revealed a glimpse of the old spirit that had accomplished so much during the Civil War:

I thank the "Master" as [General O. O.] Howard says that I am able to be at my desk each day and beside my *official* work do something to make an old veteran, or *oftener* now, a veteran's widow glad. I count the day lost that passes without having called up *one* claim, going through it and writing the claimant, though it is out of order for any *clerk* to do anything of the kind--but I am an irregular somebody as you know. I am often called to account for my irregularities, but always excused.

Sarah spent 23 years in Washington, continuing to work in the Pension Office until shortly before her death on December 22, 1907. She was buried at Arlington on Christmas Day.

The stately granite marker erected over her grave reads:

SARAH S. SAMPSON
Volunteer Nurse
Civil War
Wife of
CHAS. A. L. SAMPSON
Lt. Col. 3d Maine Col. Inf.

And a small bronze tablet, now weathered to verdigris, is

attached to the base of the stone, the final gesture of those old soldiers who remained to the end her grateful patients:

THIS TABLET IS
DEDICATED IN LOVING
MEMORY TO
SARAH S. SAMPSON
BY THE
THIRD MAINE REGIMENT
ASSOCIATION

Photo by FAYE HARRISON
SARAH'S GRAVE AT ARLINGTON

[80]

CHAPTER IV

CONCLUSION

". . . [T]hey exhibited a like persistence, endurance, and faith. . . ."
--FRANK MOORE

While the reunited Union struggled to find a way back to some kind of national normalcy, the individuals who had survived the war were working toward the same kind of personal goal. The hope was that this would not only be possible, but perhaps even effortless. The July 8, 1865, minutes of the Maine Camp Hospital Association welcomed home their last female representative from the fields of battle in Virginia with the declaration that its members would "follow her to the common pursuits of life."

For some--perhaps even many--of the women nurses of the Civil War this is very likely what happened. For others it is clearly not. Several of the women died during or soon after their service, from illness and exhaustion. Others returned from the war to a world so changed there was no possibility that they would ever "tak[e] up again the daily routine." Among the latter were Sarah Sampson and Isabella Fogg. The Civil War left both Isabella and Hugh Fogg hopelessly crippled; Charles Sampson came home chronically ill, doomed to an early death; Sarah's burden, though infinitely easier to bear than those of the others, was lasting: she could never forget the men and their needs and concerns.

But Sarah and Isabella were strong women. They had defied convention and prejudice to go to a war and to take care of men there, and doing so they had seen and endured horrors almost beyond imagination. After the war, they fought on--for their survival and the survival of those they loved--and they did so as long as they lived. These two women from Maine have left for all of us lessons in courage and love, and, perhaps most important of all, they contributed immeasurably to the enduring legacy of the tender and proud profession of nursing.

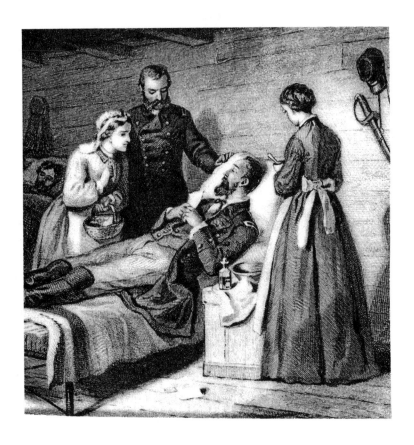

The Women Who Went to the Field

The following poem, composed by Clara Barton, was read by her at the Farewell Reception and Banquet of the Ladies of the Potomac Corps held at Williard's Hotel, Washington, D.C., on November 18, 1892. The poem was a response to a toast: "To the women who went to the field."

The women who went to the field, you say,
The women who went to the field; and pray
What did they go for?--just to be in the way?
They'd not know the difference betwixt work and
      play,
And what did they know about war, anyway?
What could they do? of what use could they be?
They would scream at the sight of a gun, don't you
      see?
Just fancy them round where the bugle-notes play,
And the long roll is bidding us on to the fray.
Imagine their skirts 'mong artillery wheels,
And watch for their flutter as they flee 'cross the
      fields
When the charge is rammed home and the fire
      belches hot;
They never would wait for the answering shot.
They would faint at the first drop of blood in their
      sight.
What fun for us boys--(ere we enter the fight);

They might pick some lint, and tear up some sheets,
And make us some jellies, and send on their sweets,
And knit some soft socks for Uncle Sam's shoes,
And write us some letters, and tell us the news.
And thus it was settled, by common consent,
Of husbands, or brothers, or whoever went,
That the place for the women was in their own
    homes,
There to patiently wait until victory comes.
But later it chanced----just how, no one knew--
That the lines slipped a bit, some began to crowd
    through;
And they went--where did they go? --Ah! where
    did they not?
Show us the battle, the field, or the spot
Where the groans of the wounded rang out on the
    air
That her ear caught it not, and her hand was not
    there;
Who wiped the death sweat from the cold, clammy
    brow,
And sent home the message: "'Tis well with him
    now";
Who watched in the tents while the fever fires
    burned,
And pain-tossing limbs in agony turned,
And wet the parched tongue, calmed delirium's strife
Till the dying lips murmured, "My mother," "My
    wife"?
And who were they all? --They were many, my men;
Their records were kept by no tabular pen;
They exist in traditions from father to son,
Who recalls, in dim memory, now here and there
    one.
A few names were writ, and by chance live today;
But's a perishing record, fast fading away.
Of those we recall, there are scarcely two score--
Dix, Dame, Bickerdyke, Edson, Harvey, and Moore--
Fales, Wittemeyer, Gilson, Safford, and Lee,

And poor Cutter, dead in the sands of the sea;
And Frances D. Gage, our "Aunt Fanny" of old,
Whose voice rang for freedom when freedom was
        sold.
And Husband, and Etheridge, and Harlan and
        Case,
Livermore, Alcott, Hancock, and Chase,
And Turner, and Hawley, and Potter, and Hall.
Ah! the list grows apace, as they come at the call;
Did these women quail at the sight of a gun?
Will some soldier tell us of one he saw run?
Will he glance at the boats on the great western
        flood,
At Pittsburg and Shiloh, did they faint at the blood?
And the brave wife of Grant stood there with them
        then,
And her calm stately presence gave strength to his
        men.
And Marie of Logan: she went with them too;
A bride, scarcely more than a sweetheart, it's true.
Her young cheek grows pale when the bold troopers
        ride,
Where the "Black Eagle" soars she is close at his
        side.
She stanches his blood, cools the fever-burnt breath,
And the wave of her hand stays the Angel of Death;
She nurses him back, and restores once again
To both army and state the great leader of men.
She has smoothed his black plumes and laid them to
        sleep,
While the angels above them their high vigils keep;
And she sits there alone, with the snow on her brow--
Your cheers for her, Comrades! Three cheers for
        her now--
And these were the women who went to the war:
The women of question: *What did they go for?*
Because in their hearts God had planted the seed
Of pity for woe, and help for its need;

They saw, in high purpose, a duty to do,
And the armor of right broke the barriers through.
Uninvited, unaided, unsanctioned ofttimes,
With pass, or without it, they pressed on the lines;
They pressed, they implored, till they ran the lines
       through,
And that was the "running" the men saw them do.
'Twas hampered work, its worth largely lost;
It was hindrance and pain, and effort, and cost:
But through these came knowledge--and knowledge is
       power,
And never again in the deadliest hour
Of war or of peace shall we be so beset
To accomplish the purpose our spirits have met.
And what would they do if war came again?
The scarlet cross floats where all was blank then.
They would pin on their "brassards" and march to
       the fray,
And the man liveth not who could say to them nay;
They would stand with you now, as they stood with
       you then--
The nurses--consolers and saviors of men.

ENDNOTES

CHAPTER I: *INTRODUCTION*

Cover: Quotation from Harriet Eaton's journal, May 4, 1863, recorded in The *Semi-Annual Report of the Maine Camp Hospital Association of Portland*, Collection S-1, Pamphlet 62, and referred to below as *MCHA* (Portland: N. A. Foster & Co., Printers, 1863), p. 22, at the Maine Historical Society in Portland (referred to below as *MHS*). **Photo** of Harriet Whetten courtesy of the Wisconsin State Historical Society; ". . .[S]he has discarded hoops. . . ." from *Woman's Work in the Civil War*, L. P. Brockett and Mary C. Vaughan (Philadelphia: Zeigler, McCurdy & Co., 1867), p. 291; ". . . [A] steamer came alongside. . . ." from "A Volunteer Nurse in the Civil War: The Letters of Harriet Douglas Whetten," ed. Paul H. Hass, *Wisconsin Magazine of History*, Winter, 1964-1965 [pp. 131-151], p. 145. **Page 1**: "I am not accustomed. . . ." Lincoln's words about women from *Noble Women of the North*, ed. Sylvia G. Dannett (London: Thomas Yoseloff, 1943), p. 398. **Page 2**: Florence Nightingale's words "every woman is a nurse" are from her *Notes on Nursing* (Edinburgh: Churchill Livingston, rpt. 1980), p. *v* of Preface; long quotation from Marjorie Barstow Greenbie's *Lincoln's Daughters of Mercy* (New York: G. P. Putnam's Sons, 1944), p. 51. **Page 3**: "I ride over the battlefield. . . ." from John Beatty, *Memoirs of a Volunteer 1861-1863* (New York: W. W. Norton & Company, Inc., 1946), p. 159. **Page 4**: Kate Scott's long quotation is from the introduction of a pamphlet (referred to below as *NAAN*) produced in honor of the National Association of Civil War Nurses by the Grand Army of the Republic for its 44th Encampment in 1910. **Page 5**: Numbers of doctors from "Calamity and Sanitation" by John E. DiMeglio, *The Social Studies*, Vol. 65, No. 2, Feb. 1974 [pp. 75-82], p. 77. Volume Seven, *Prisons and Hospitals*, of the ten-volume series *The Photographic History of Civil the War*, ed. Holland Thompson (New York: The Review of Reviews Co., 1911), asserts (pp. 220-223) that at the beginning of the war the "Medical Department of the regular army" consisted of one surgeon general at the rank of colonel, 30 surgeons with the rank of major, and 84 assistant surgeons with the rank of first lieutenant and (after five years) captain--for a total of 115. Soon 27 resigned--24 to join the CSA--leaving a total of 88 doctors in the Union army. **Page 6**: Long quotation from Mary Livermore, *My Story of the War* (Hartford: Worthington and Company, 1889), p. 202; "The principle of active war is. . . ." from Katharine Wormeley, *The Other Side of War* (Boston: Ticknor and Co., 1889), p. 150; "miserable holes. . . ." from Harriet Eaton's diaries in the Southern Historical Collection, Wilson Library, University of North Carolina at Chapel Hill, Volume 2 (referred to below as *Eaton Diary*). **Page 7**: ". . . Bridgeport, Connecticut. . . ." from Greenbie, p. 7; ". . . very early to the front.

. . ." from a letter written by Mrs. William S. Preble to Frank Moore, dated April 9, 1866 (in the Frank Moore Papers in the Special Collections Library, Duke University [referred to below as *SCL, Duke*]). **Page 8**: "The women must be over thirty. . . ." Livermore, p. 246; "No lady . . . should attempt to come. . . ." from Wormeley, p. 127; "Your disapprobation has been. . . ." from Hass, p. 140; "I struggled long and hard. . . ." from Stephen B. Oates, *A Woman of Valor* (New York: The Free Press, 1994), p. 374. **Page 9**: The long quotation at top of page is from Sarah A. Palmer, *The Story of Aunt Becky's Army Life* (New York: John F. Trow & Co., 1867), p. 1; "[s]cores of young maidens. . . ." from the introduction of *NAAN*. **Page 10**: "I kept no daily journal. . . ." in a letter from Isabella Fogg to Frank Moore, March 17, 1866 (*SCL, Duke*). **Page 11**: ". . . [W]e was an awful dirty set. . . ." from a letter to Frank Moore from George Brown, Jan. 3, 1866 (*SCL, Duke*); there is much evidence that the Civil War nurse thought of the soldiers as family: "Administering medicines & food and caring for them in every way as if they were our brothers is what I have to do. . . ." Hass, p. 139; long quotation from John R. Brumgardt, *Civil War Nurse: The Diary and Letters of Hannah Ropes* (Univ. of Tenn. Press, 1980), p. 33. **Page 12**: "He's a Rebel. . . ." from Wormeley, p. 170; long quotation is from E. W. Locke, *Three Years in Camp and Hospital* (Boston: George D. Russell & Co., 1872), p. 184.

CHAPTER II: MAINE MOTHER AT WAR

Page 13: Poem is from Charles A. Humpreys, *Field, Camp, Hospital and Prison in the Civil War, 1863-1865* (New York: Books for Libraries Press, rpt. 1971), p. 11; biographical information about Isabella Fogg is from the authors' March 1996 interview with Mr. and Mrs. Brand Livingstone; although several letters survive with Isabella Fogg's signature on them, it appears that these were all dictated, or are copies made by a clerk--it is not certain that she ever, for whatever reason, maintained her own correspondence. **Page 15**: Long quotation is from Frank Moore, *Women and War: Their Heroism and Self-Sacrifice* (Hartford: S. S. Scranton & Co., 1866), p. 113. **Page 17**: The information about Hugh Fogg's physical characteristics is from his military records and pension file at the National Archives (referred to below as *NA*) in Washington, D.C.; Captain (later Major) Haycock's Company B of the First Battalion, Sixth Infantry Volunteers was a state organization which became a part of the United States Army as of July 15, 1861, as Company D, Sixth Maine Infantry (*NA*); the ages of the men in Company D from Calais are listed, individually, in James H. Mundy, *No Rich Men's Sons* (Cape Elizabeth, Maine: Harp Publications, 1994), pp. 238-242; "a splendid set of men. . . ." from the *Portland Advertiser* and quoted in Mundy, p.

29; "They are large men. . . ." from a letter written by G. W. Dyer to Gov. Coburn, June 27, 1861, in the Maine State Archives, in Augusta (referred to below as *MSA*). **Page 18**: In a July 8, 1861, letter to Gov. Coburn (*MSA*), Dyer writes that "The Calais company were furnished by their town with shirts, trousers, shoes, hats and underclothing, stockings. . . ."; Isabella's experience in Annapolis in Moore, p. 114. **Page 19**: "The mutilated heroes. . . ." and long quotation from Moore, p. 115. **Page 22**: The phrase "some of the very best men" is from Mundy, p. 80. **Page 23**: Information about the origin of the Maine Camp Hospital Association is from a flier in Collection S-61, and additional information is available in *MCHA*, p. 1. **Page 24**: The quotation in the caption of the photograph is from an undated flier, "To the People of Maine," in Collection S-61 (*MHS*). **Page 25**: The long quotation *MCHA*, p. 7; the quotation ". . . instructed to administer to all. . . ." from brochure in Collection S-61 (*MHS*); *Eaton Diary*, Oct. 6, 1862. **Page 27**: Letter to Colonel Hathaway written Nov. 10, 1862 (*MSA*); long quotation from letter found in *MCHA*, pp. 4-5. **Page 28**: "I find . . . that Mrs. Fogg works. . . ." from Dec. 22, 1862, letter (*MSA*); possible causes for her dismissal from "Civil War Nurse Gets Recognition," by Tess Nacelewicz, *Maine Sunday Telegram*, Aug. 14, 1994, p. 12B; Hayes decision to go with Isabella stated in his Dec. 22, 1862, letter (*MSA*); the handwriting of Isabella's letter to Dyer is Eaton's. **Page 31**: Letter at *MSA*; independent information about Alden Litchfield's personality can be found in Theodore Gerrish, *Army Life* (Portland: Hoyt, Fogg & Donham, 1882), pp. 69-71, and *Eaton Diary*, Jan. 21, 1863: "That Quartermaster Litchfield of Rockland is in my opinion a great rascal, a man void entirely of principal. . . ." **Page 32**: March 18, 1863, and April 17, 1863, entries from *Eaton Diary*. **Page 34**: May 1, 1863, entry from *Eaton Diary*; phrase "as they came pouring from the field," Moore p. 121; May 3, 1863, entry from *Eaton Diary*; first part of long quotation is from flier found in Collection S-61 (*MHS*); second part of this long quotation is from *MCHA*, p. 7. **Page 35**: Letter from Dr. Holmes in Isabella Fogg's pension file (*NA*). **Page 36**: Information about Isabella's movements from Moore, p. 123; information about Hugh's from his pension file (*NA*); information about Isabella's disassociation from the MCHA from Nacelewicz, p. 12B. **Page 37**: Chamberlain's letter and the letter quoted at length are from Isabella's pension file (*NA*); information about Isabella's visit to Maine and her grant from the legislature is from her pension file (*NA*). **Page 39**: Hugh Fogg's diagnosis found in his military records (*NA*); in *Disease in the Civil War*, by Paul E. Steiner (Springfield, Ill.: Charles C. Thomas, 1968), p. 222, is the following: "The occurrence of so much smallpox in the second half of the war despite the regulation requiring vaccination reflects both carelessness and resistance to the procedure"; information about smallpox vaccinations in

Washington, D.C., from Shirley Blotnick Moskow, *Emma's World* (Far Hills, New Jersey: New Horizon Press, 1990), p. 194: "The law has been passed causing all who have not been inoculated for five years to proceed immediately to a doctor or suffer a serious penalty. . . . Would it not be awful if it should get into the army?"; for a fuller discussion of smallpox, smallpox vaccination and syphilis, see George Worthington Adams, *Doctors in Blue* (Dayton: Morningside, 1985), pp. 219-220, and "rusty pins. . . ." is from p. 220 (one conclusion drawn after certain cases of "syphilis" were reexamined: "The majority of the investigators decided against syphilis as a diagnosis, and tended to lay the difficulties to incipient scurvy. . . ."); information about prostitutes is from Oates, p. 212; anonymous letter found in *SCL, Duke*. **Page 40**: Chamberlain quoted in Oates, p. 114; the phrase "toiling day and night without sleep" from Oates, p. 237; "It was indescribable. . . ." Moore, p. 124; Isabella's activities from her pension file (*NA*); information about Hugh's unit from the Maine State *Adjutant General's Report for the Year . . . 1866* (Augusta: Stevens & Sayward, Printers to the State, 1867), p. 27 and Hugh Fogg's military records (*NA*). **Page 42**: Phrase "sent to make reports" from Isabella's pension file (*NA*); long quotation written by John William DeFoult, quoted in Thomas A. Lewis, *The Guns of Cedar Creek* (New York: Harper & Row, New York, 1988), p. 288; Hugh's wound could have been affected by traumatic erysipelas, "an extremely contagious streptococcal infection" which spread quickly, a "repulsive and feared disease" which was known as "hospital gangrene" (from H. H. Cunningham, *Doctors in Gray* [Baton Rouge: Louisiana State University Press, 1958), pp. 238-239; the number of Federals wounded from Lewis, p. 288. **Page 44**: Details of Hugh's surgery from his pension file in the National Archives; Isabella's activities from her pension file (*NA*); Isabella's activities during this period found in her pension file (*NA*), as well as statement of her condition, "completely helpless for upwards. . . ." **Page 45**: Quotation as caption is from James I. Robertson, Jr., *Tenting Tonight* (Alexandria, Virginia: Time-Life Books, 1984), p. 94. **Page 46**: Letter from Isabella (long quotation) concerning Hugh's hospitalization in Hugh's pension file (*NA*) ; "I was entirely confined to my bed. . . ." from letter written by Isabella to Moore, April 11, 1866 (*SCL, Duke*). **Page 47**: Caption is from letter written by Chamberlain, in Isabella's pension file (*NA*). **Page 48**: Pension information from Isabella's pension file (*NA*); information that Isabella was the *only women of the Civil War granted . . . pension* is from Nacelewicz, 12B; "extreme helplessness & poverty" from a letter written by Edward P. Smith to Moore, May 31, 1866 (*SCL, Duke*); "During my sufferings. . . ." from a March 17, 1866, letter written to Moore by Isabella (*SCL*); information about Isabella's pension from her file (*NA*). **Page 49**: Information about Isabella's pension is from her file (*NA*); information about Hugh's discharge, marriage, employment, and death is from his pension file (*NA*). **Page 50**: Isabella's apparently quoted words from Moore, p. 126.

Chapter III: *SARAH SERVED*

Page 51: Lines from Will Carleton's "Cover Them Over" quoted from his *Farm Legends* (New York: Harper & Brothers, 1876), p. 89. **Page 52**: Biographical information about Sarah and Charles Sampson is from Lawrence M. Sturtevant's *Sarah Sampson and the Third Maine Regiment of Volunteers in the Civil War 1861-1865: A Documentary History*, undated (one of three typed manuscripts; the one the authors consulted is located at the Bath Historical Society (referred to below as *BHS*); "because my husband was called to the front. . . ." from *The Bath Independent*, August 18, 1906, p. 1. **Page 54**: Dr. Garcelon identified by Sturtevant, p. 13, who writes that he "was in the field at First Bull Run" onward; Sarah's letter to Dr. Garcelon is in the Maine State Archives (*MSA*) at Augusta. **Page 55**: The long quotation is from the same June 14th letter to Dr. Garcelon (*MSA*). **Page 56**: "Mrs. Sampson is one of the best. . . ." from a June 29, 1861, letter written by Howard to his wife Lizzie--found in Sturtevant, p. 29 (original in the O. O. Howard Collection at Bowdoin College); Volume One of *Autobiography of Oliver Otis Howard* (Freeport, New York: Books for Libraries Press, 1971 rpt. of 1907), p. 137; "I wrote a long letter to his wife. . . ." from a letter written by Sarah to Howard on Oct. 22, 1861--found in Sturtevant, p. 38 (original in the O. O. Howard Collection at Bowdoin College); ". . . I am perfectly well. . . ." from Sarah's June 14th letter to Garcelon (*MSA*). **Page 57**: Sarah's account of her meeting President Lincoln is from the *Bath Independent and Enterprise*, August 8, 1906, p. 5; the account of Sarah's experiences as a Civil War nurse is from her own report, "Mrs. [Sarah] Sampson's Report" in *Report of the Adjutant General of Maine, 1864-1865* (Augusta: Stevens & Sayward, Printers to the State), pp. 108-128, referred to below as *Sarah's Report*. **Page 58**: "My sick soldiers. . . ." *Sarah's Report*, p. 110 *Sarah was at White House landing. . . .* and "hearing that Hooker's division. . . ." *Sarah's Report*, p. 111. **Page 60**: "The estimated four thousand. . . ." John M. Coski, *The Army of the Potomac at Berkeley Plantation: The Harrison Landing Occupation of 1862*, 1982, p. 4; Sarah's long quotation from *Sarah's Report*, p. 112; long quotation at bottom of page from Wormeley, pp. 103-104. **Page 62**: Phrase "one of the most demoralizing" from Coski, p. 5; "indelible disgrace: and "prompted by cowardice. . . ." from Coski, p. 4; "enough to melt the heart. . . ." Coski, p. 5. **Page 63**: Information about Charles and Sarah from Sarah's pension file (*NA*); "He has lost none. . . ." from July 10, 1862, letter (*MSA*); "I am so anxious to learn. . . ." August 1, 1862 (*MSA*). **Page 64**: Sept. 2, 1862, letter (at length) from "Ladies" (*MSA*). **Page**

65: "I proceeded to Washington. . . ." *Sarah's Report*, p. 113; information Sarah's daily hospital visits from *Sarah's Report*, p. 114. **Page 66**: Caption from William Howell Reed, *Hospital Life in the Army of the Potomac* (Boston: William V. Spencer, 1866), p. 144. **Page 68**: Journal entry from *Sarah's Report*, pp. 119-120. **Page 69**: Long quotation ending on first line of this page from *Sarah's Report*, p. 125; Rebecca Usher's Diary, Collection 9 (*MHS*). **Page 70**: Long quotation at bottom from *Sarah's Report*, p. 125. **Page 71**: Caption from Sarah's letter of July 13, 1861, at *MHS*. **Page 72**: Title from the dedication of Livermore; caption from *Sarah's Report*, p. 127. **Page 73**: letter from patient at Harewood at *MHS*; letters from Sarah to Hodsdon of July 13 & 18, 1864, at *MSA*. **Page 74**: Sarah's Dec. 9, 1864, letter at *MSA*; "An order having been issued. . . ." *Sarah's Report*, pp. 126-127. **Page 75**: Long quotation from top from Moore, p. 461; "The entire camp. . . ." *Sarah's Report*, p. 127; "the ground was covered" Moore, p. 462; "distributing supplies" from *Sarah's Report*, pp. 127-128. **Page 77**: Sarah's immediate postwar activities from her pension file (*NA*); information about the orphan home from Gordon Struble, "Gordon's Gleanings," *Bath Historical Society Newsletter*, No. 8, Sept.-Oct. 1990 (*BHS*); *The Times Record* of Brunswick, Maine, reported on May 1, 1996 (p. 1), that the orphan home which Sarah founded was "out of compliance" and too expensive to repair and would be closed. It was the last staterun home for children in Maine. **Page 78**: Words "sweet-faced" and "gracious" from *Bath Independent Enterprise*, August 8, 1906, p. 5 (*BHS*); information about Sarah's pension from her file at *NA*; "quiet, constant attendant" and "Florence Nightingale of Maine" from *Bath Daily Times*, Dec. 29, 1907, p. 3 (*BHS*); "idol" from *Bath Independent Enterprise*, Dec. 23, 1907, p. 1 (*BHS*). **Page 79**: Sarah's May 21, 1900, letter to Chamberlain at *MHS*; her Nov. 21, 1900, letter at *MHS*.

CHAPTER IV: *CONCLUSION*

Page 81: "The phrase "tak[e] up again the daily routine" is from Kate Scott in *NAAN*: ". . . [the nurses] went quietly to their homes, and took up again the daily routines. . . ."

BHS	BATH HISTORICAL SOCIETY
EATON DIARY	SEE NOTES FOR PAGE 6.
MCHA	SEE NOTE FOR COVER.
MHS	MAINE HISTORICAL SOCIETY, AT PORTLAND, MAINE
MSA	MAINE STATE ARCHIVES, AT AUGUSTA, MAINE
NA	NATIONAL ARCHIVES, AT WASHINGTON, D.C
NAAN	SEE NOTES FOR PAGE 4.
SCL, DUKE	SEE NOTES FOR PAGE 7.

SELECTED BIBLIOGRAPHY

Complete bibliographic information for every citation is available within the endnotes. This selected bibliography is a list of those works quoted which the reader interested in (Union) Civil War nurses might find generally most helpful.

Adams, George Worthington. *Doctors in Blue.* Dayton: Morningside, 1985.

Brockett, L. P. and Mary C. Vaughan. *Woman's Work in the Civil War.* Philadelphia: Zeigler, McCurdy & Co., 1967.

Brumgardt, John R. *Civil War Nurse: The Diary and Letters of Hannah Ropes.* University of Tennessee Press, 1980.

Cunningham, H. H. *Doctors in Gray.* Baton Rouge: Louisiana State University Press, 1958.

Dannett, Sylvia G. *Noble Women of the North.* London: Thomas Yoseloff, 1943.

Greenbie, Marjorie Barstow. *Lincoln's Daughter's of Mercy.* New York: G. P. Putnam's Sons, 1944.

Humpreys, Charles A. *Field, Camp, Hospital and Prison in the Civil War, 1863-1865.* New York: Books for Libraries Press, rpt. 1971.

Livermore, Mary Ashton. *My Story of the War.* Hartford: Worthington and Company, 1889.

Locke, E. W. *Three Years in Camp and Hospital.* Boston: George D. Russell & Co., 1872.

Moore, Frank. *Women and War: Their Heroism and Self-Sacrifice.* Hartford: S. S. Scranton & Co., 1866.

Oates, Stephen B. *Woman of Valor.* New York: The Free Press, 1994.

Thompson, Holland, ed. *Prisons and Hospitals,* Volume Seven of THE PHOTOGRAPHIC HISTORY OF THE CIVIL WAR IN TEN VOLUMES, Francis Trevelan, general ed. New York: The Review of Reviews Co., 1911.

Wormeley, Katharine. *The Other Side of War.* Boston: Ticknor and Co., 1889.